VEGETARIAN

101 RECIPES CELEBRATING FRESH, SEASONAL INGREDIENTS

ALICE HART

Photographs by Lisa Linder

MURDOCH BOOKS

SYDNEY · LONDON

Contents

Fast

One pots and bakes

Special

ESSENTIALS

Mushrooms and herbs

If you're fond of meat but want to cut down your intake, many mushrooms (notably gigantic field mushrooms) have a juicy, beefy quality that readily satisfies meat hankerings.

Golden chanterelles, delicate enoki, shaggy chestnuts and tasty porcini are just a few examples of the wide variety of mushrooms available, so celebrate the mushroom season and experiment. If culinary inspiration eludes you, just fry them in butter, garlic and herbs and enjoy them on toast. Heaven.

Herbs make cooking joyful, so treat them well. Robust rosemary, sage and bay leaves need time to meld with companions in the pot, so add them early in the cooking process. The tender likes of coriander (cilantro), parsley and basil go in at the end so their lovely oils don't dissipate.

Vegetables and fruit

It's easy to take these vegetarian staples for granted, but try not to. Tricky cooking and exotic varieties are not necessary – although I urge you to try the unfamiliar. Just buy seasonal, organic and ripe – and pause for thought if you're inclined to cook on autopilot. You don't have to steam them every time.

Have you tried sprinkling simple vegetables with toasted seeds or topping them with a knob of nut butter? It takes just moments to raise a dish from dull to delicious. And get to know your ingredients. Salad leaves have wildly different personalities that you can't appreciate if you only know them as the contents of a plastic bag.

Soulful onion and her cousin, garlic, are kingpins of the vegetarian kitchen, and come into their own when cooked gently in oil or butter, slow roasted or sweated in a pan. Pots of this sweet onion 'confit' will keep in the refrigerator ready for use in other dishes, or can be enjoyed on bread with strong cheese.

Your kitchen armoury is also lacking without lemon. A spritz here or a shower of zest there can enliven, intensify or transform all manner of sweet and savoury dishes.

Legumes

These delicious pods – including beans, lentils, peanuts, peas and soya beans – range from creamy white and dappled pink through to vivid red and smoky grey, like nature's own edible buttons and beads. Moreover, they're low in fat, high in protein and rich in nutrients, especially Vitamin Bs, iron and calcium.

Cooking legumes isn't onerous. Lentils and dried peas need no soaking. Pulses and beans do, for between 8 and 12 hours: just pour into a bowl of water before bedtime and they'll be plump and ready to cook by morning. If you forget to soak them, cover with water and boil fiercely for a few minutes and set aside for 2 hours then cook as normal. Don't bother salting the water – it toughens the skin.

Robust herbs and aromatic vegetables added to the cooking water will enhance any type of legume: then mash, purée, mould into patties or add to salads and casseroles as you wish. Slippery with flavoursome oil or flecked with herbs and spices, legumes also hold their own in the flavour stakes.

Nuts, seeds and oils

Nuts and seeds can be used in a range of culinary guises: toasted, ground, whole, sprouted, pressed into fragrant oil, whizzed into butter or transformed into milk. They can raise a dish from merely edible to one that sings with flavour, and add texture and depth of flavour to soups, casseroles and vegetables.

Nuts and seeds are tiny nutritional powerhouses: high in fibre, rich in nutrients and an excellent source of protein. The fat in nuts is now known to be largely mono or polyunsaturated – that's the good stuff – so they find favour with nutritionists. In any event, only modest amounts are needed to impart substance to cooking.

Try using rich nut and seed oils in cold food or to anoint steamed vegetables, or add them to hot dishes at the eleventh hour so the piquancy is not destroyed by cooking. (Do give special oils a place of honour in a dark cupboard to preserve freshness.) Or, whizz up almonds, pecans, cashews, hazelnuts or macadamias into creamy nut 'butters'. You can also blend various seeds to make mouth-tingling sprinkles.

Rice and grains

Rice and grains are comforting, economical, delicious and nutritious, as well as being the starting point for countless dishes and products as varied as wine, milk, pasta and noodles.

Know the basics and you can choose the most appropriate rice for your purpose. Thin and dainty long-grains stay separated after cooking and make fluffy beds for curries and sauces. Short- and medium-grains are plumper and starchier and stick together when cooked. Medium-grain rice is used in dishes like paella; short-grains makes creamy puddings and risottos.

Brown rice and wild rice (a misnomer, as it's actually a grain) require more patience to cook than white rice, but the nutty, earthy flavours are worth the extra effort. Please forage in your health food shop and invite more of the unfamiliar grains into your kitchen: quinoa, amaranth, barley, burghul (bulgur)...

Decanting rice and grain into airtight containers is not just for those who like their cupboards neat: it helps prevent them going rancid. Remember that cooked rice or grain left at room temperature can encourage bacteria to multiply, so serve when just cooked or refrigerate within 1 hour of cooking.

Dairy and eggs

Milk, butter, cream, cheese and yoghurt are the cornerstone ingredients of desserts and baking, but also have a special place in vegetarian kitchens. A swirl of cream in soup, a gloss-inducing knob of butter in sauce, or parings of salty cheese on salad leaves: these add richness to food that might be otherwise underwhelming. A globe of burrata or oven-baked ricotta cheese will never leave a carnivore feeling deprived.

There are so many options. Some cheeses are divine eaten raw, others are meltingly transformed by heat. Yoghurt can evolve into cheese such as labne: made in a muslin mould, it emerges striated with markings and is beautiful to behold as well as eat. Some ingredients in this book, such as parmesan, are made from animal rennet, but alternatives suitable for vegetarians are readily available, so substitute if you wish.

Eggs add substance to a non-meat meal because they're packed with protein and are therefore filling. But they are sensitive to heat and can be tricky to cook. The key is not to overcook them. For the best flavour, sunniest yolks and thickest whites, opt for free-range and organic eggs when possible.

Almond milk has such a delicate, pure sweetness that it makes a beautiful porridge. I favour this raw, but on cold days hot porridge is really the only option, so heat it through gently. You can, of course, make porridge with other milks in place of the almond milk.

Almond milk and maple porridge

SERVES 4
PREPARATION TIME: 10 MINUTES
PLUS SOAKING TIME
COOKING TIME: 5 MINUTES

200g (7oz) rolled oats

½ a small cinnamon stick

500ml (17floz) fresh, unsweetened almond milk (see page 20)

50g (1¾oz) medjool dates, pitted and chopped

50g (1¾oz) flaked almonds, lightly toasted

a drizzle of maple syrup

If you can, soak the oats and cinnamon in half the almond milk the night before and keep in the refrigerator overnight. The oats will soften beautifully, enough to be eaten just as they are with the chopped dates, flaked almonds and a little maple syrup.

To cook the porridge, transfer the oat mixture to a saucepan with the remaining almond milk. Heat gently, stirring constantly for a few minutes until the porridge turns thick and creamy. Add a little water if it looks too thick.

Remove the cinnamon stick and divide the oats among four warmed bowls. Top with the dates, almonds and a drizzle of maple syrup.

Starting this recipe the night before will result in delicious plump oats that have soaked up all the milk. You could use walnut or soy milk here instead of cow's milk, and a mild honey instead of the agave nectar. Or just use diluted fruit juice instead.

Pear and walnut bircher muesli

SERVES 2
PREPARATION TIME: 10 MINUTES
PLUS SOAKING TIME

2 firm pears, coarsely grated

a squeeze of lemon

120g (4¼oz) rolled oats

2 tablespoons mixed seeds

2 tablespoons chopped walnuts

1 tablespoon agave nectar

100ml (3½floz) fresh pear or apple juice

100ml (3½floz) milk or water

1-2 tablespoons plain yoghurt, plus extra to serve

a few walnut halves and fresh pear slices, to serve

The night before, toss the grated pears with the lemon juice to stop them browning and combine with the oats, seeds and 1 tablespoon of the chopped walnuts in a large bowl. Add the agave nectar, pear or apple juice, and the milk or water. Stir well, cover and refrigerate.

The following morning, stir in a spoonful of yoghurt and the remaining chopped walnuts. Divide between two bowls and top with extra yoghurt, walnut halves and fresh pear slices.

If you can spare 15 minutes, delicious melty panini can be yours for breakfast instead of a sad bowl of bran flakes. Wrap them in paper to keep warm for 10 minutes – this will give you just enough time to run for the bus before you tuck in.

Toasted goat's curd and charred tomato panini

MAKES 2 PANINI
READY IN 15 MINUTES

2 small ciabatta rolls

1 large, ripe tomato, sliced 5mm (¼in) thick

75g (2½oz) soft, mild goat's curd

3 tarragon sprigs, leaves only

olive oil, for drizzling

Split each ciabatta in half horizontally. If the rolls are very thick, slice them into three pieces and save the middle section for breadcrumbs, leaving you with thin top and bottom pieces.

Place a non-stick frying pan over a high heat until smoking hot. Add the tomato to the pan, making sure the end pieces are cut side down. Leave undisturbed for a minute before reducing the heat to medium and leaving to char for a further minute or so. Remove from the pan with a spatula and set aside.

Beat the goat's curd and tarragon together and spread over the bottom ciabatta halves. Put the tomatoes onto the curd mixture, and place the remaining ciabatta halves on top, pressing them down firmly. Drizzle the tops and bottoms of the panini with a little olive oil.

Switch on an electric sandwich press if you have one, or place a sturdy chargrill pan on the stove to heat. If using a sandwich press, place the panini on the hotplate and press the lid down to flatten the panini as they cook. Cook for at least 2 minutes, or according to your machine's instructions. If using a chargrill pan, place the panini in the hot pan and rest a heavy frying pan on top to weigh them down. Cook over a medium-high heat for 1–2 minutes then remove the frying pan, turn the panini over and replace the pan to weigh them down for a further 1 minute. Whichever way you cook the panini, eat while they're still warm.

Versatile recipes such as this antipasto favourite don't like to be pigeon-holed – herb and chilli-flecked baked ricotta can be served as breakfast, brunch, lunch or supper. The richly sweet and smoky compote is an excellent foil for the creamy cheese.

Baked ricotta with avocado

SERVES 4
PREPARATION TIME: 15 MINUTES
COOKING TIME: 20-25 MINUTES

500g (1lb2oz) ricotta cheese, drained

2 tablespoons finely grated pecorino or parmesan cheese

1 red chilli, seeded and finely chopped

2 tablespoons chopped basil

2 eggs, lightly beaten

extra virgin olive oil, to oil and drizzle

4 thick slices sourdough bread, toasted

2 ripe avocados, sliced

1 bunch rocket (arugula)

For the capsicum compote

3 red capsicums (peppers)

3 long red chillies

1 red onion, halved and thinly sliced

2 tablespoons olive oil

1 garlic clove, crushed

1 tablespoon light brown sugar

3 tablespoons sherry vinegar

a pinch of sweet smoked paprika

To make the compote, blacken the capsicums and chillies over a gas flame or under a very hot grill (broiler), turning with tongs every minute or so until charred all over. Transfer to a bowl, cover with plastic wrap and set aside for a few minutes. Scrape the blackened skin from the capsicums and chillies, halve them and scrape out the seeds. Roughly chop the flesh and set aside.

Gently fry the onion in the olive oil until softened then reduce the heat and add the garlic and chopped capsicums. Cook for 5 minutes more then add the sugar, vinegar and paprika and cook until caramelised. Spoon into a sterilised jar and chill until needed.

Preheat the oven to 190°C (375°F/Gas 5). Beat the drained ricotta, pecorino or parmesan, chilli, basil and eggs together and season with plenty of freshly ground black pepper and a little salt. Lightly oil 4 x 180ml (6floz) ovenproof ramekins or a small ovenproof dish and fill with the ricotta mixture. Bake for 20 minutes if using individual ramekins or about 25 minutes if using a single dish. Set aside to rest for a few minutes before running a knife around the edge of the dish and turning out.

Squish the baked ricotta onto the toasted sourdough, drizzle with olive oil and accompany with slices of avocado, rocket and capsicum compote.

The blackberry milkshake is arguably the less virtuous recipe here, but is so delicious. Use frozen yoghurt - plain, vanilla or berry - or, if your milkshake is more of a treat, replace the yoghurt with a scoop of vanilla ice cream and a couple of teaspoons of sugar instead of honey.

Blackberry milkshake
Mango and cashew smoothie

MAKES 2 OF EACH
PREPARATION TIME: 10 MINUTES FOR EACH
PLUS SOAKING TIME FOR THE SMOOTHIE

For the blackberry milkshake

1 vanilla bean

300g (10½oz) blackberries, fresh or frozen

a generous drizzle of mild honey

2 large scoops frozen yoghurt

400ml (14floz) milk, chilled

For the mango and cashew smoothie

100g (3½oz) unsalted cashews

300ml (10½floz) water, chilled

1 ripe mango, chopped

1 small banana

3 ice cubes, crushed

1 tablespoon golden linseeds

1 tablespoon rolled oats

BLACKBERRY MILKSHAKE
Split the vanilla bean lengthways and scrape the seeds into a blender with the tip of the knife. (You can use the empty pod to flavour a bag of sugar in your pantry.) Add the rest of the ingredients to the blender and simply blitz together. Immediately divide between two tall glasses.

MANGO AND CASHEW SMOOTHIE
Start the evening before: soak the cashews in plenty of cold water and leave overnight to soften. The following morning, drain the cashews and place in a blender with 100ml (3½floz) of the chilled water. Blitz until a paste forms then pour in a further 200ml (7floz) chilled water while the motor is running to form rich, smooth milk. This will take a couple of minutes. Add the remaining ingredients and blitz for at least another minute until smooth. Pour into two tall glasses and drink straight away.

Delicious nut milks, seed milks or nut-and-seed milks will last well for up to 3 days if kept chilled. Adding warm water and linseeds when blending the milk helps it to emulsify evenly, making it luxuriously creamy and smooth.

How to make nut milk

100g

8 hours

nuts

rub

450ml

linseeds

step 1

Put 100g (3½oz) of your choice of shelled nuts and/or seeds in a large bowl, cover with plenty of cold water and leave to soak in a cool place overnight, or for at least 8 hours. The nuts and/or seeds will soften and plump up.

step 2

If the milk is destined for a refined recipe, or if you want it to be particularly smooth, remove any skins that remain on the nuts after their soaking time. Almonds are easy to skin by blanching – just nick with a knife and slip out the white nuts. Other nuts such as walnuts and pecans will need to be vigorously rubbed with a clean tea towel to remove as much skin as possible.

step 3

Put the soaked nuts in a blender and add 450ml (16floz) warm water. Add 1 tablespoon ground linseeds to help the milk emulsify (this is not essential). Blend on a high speed for a couple of minutes until very smooth.

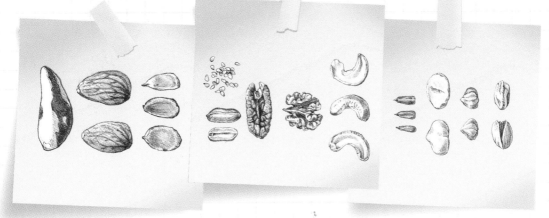

Brazil nuts, almonds, pumpkins seeds, sesame seeds, peanuts, walnuts, cashews, sunflower seeds, macadamias, hazelnuts and pistachios are all good choices on their own or in combination, but do make sure your nuts and seeds are unroasted and buy organic if possible.

step 4

Line a sieve with two layers of muslin and set the sieve over a bowl. Pour the milk through slowly to filter out the remaining nut pieces.

step 5

Gather up the muslin and squeeze it over the bowl to extract all of the liquid from the solids.

step 6

You can sweeten the nut milk with 1-2 tablespoons maple syrup, mild honey, unrefined sugar or a few pitted dates. To do this, return the milk to the rinsed blender, add the sweetener and blend again. Don't add anything more if the milk is to be used in savoury recipes, or in smoothies or shakes, as they will be sweetened as you make them. You could also add vanilla seeds, ground cinnamon, ground nutmeg or cocoa powder at this stage. Dilute with extra water if you wish. Chill and store in the fridge.

These are delicate little bites but the cheese does lend them substance. Silverbeet (Swiss chard) is related to beetroot and has an earthier taste than spinach. You could just use spinach leaves instead of silverbeet, in which case use 150g (5½oz) English spinach.

Silverbeet and brie mini muffins

MAKES 12-24
PREPARATION TIME: 20 MINUTES
COOKING TIME: 20 MINUTES

25g (1oz) butter, melted, plus extra for greasing

150g (5½oz) rainbow or green silverbeet (Swiss chard), leaves washed and shredded, stalks reserved

190g (6¾oz) self-raising flour

2 tablespoons finely grated parmesan cheese

a good grating of nutmeg

175ml (5½floz) milk

1 small egg, beaten

75g (2½oz) brie or camembert cheese, cubed

Preheat the oven to 190°C (375°F/Gas 5). Grease a 12-hole standard muffin tin or a 24-hole mini-muffin tin with a little butter or line with paper cases if you prefer.

Chop the silverbeet stalks and steam for 4 minutes, add the silverbeet leaves and steam for a further minute or so. Turn into a clean tea towel and squeeze out any excess water.

Mix the flour, 1 tablespoon of the parmesan, a pinch of salt and the nutmeg in a bowl. In a separate bowl, beat the milk, melted butter and egg together. Tip the milk mixture into the flour mixture and stir a couple of times. Now add the cooked silverbeet and the brie or camembert. Don't over-mix or the muffins will be tough – a few lumps are just fine.

Spoon the mixture into the holes of the muffin tin, sprinkle with the remaining parmesan and bake for about 15 minutes until risen and golden. Cool on wire racks or eat warm.

Black vinegar should be easy to source at Asian grocery stores, but if you don't have the means or inclination, try 2 tablespoons of rice vinegar instead. The wonton wrappers can be a little fiddly, but the wrapping gets easier as you go along, and the results are well worth it.

Potsticker dumplings with black vinegar dipping sauce

MAKES ABOUT 36
PREPARATION TIME: 20 MINUTES
COOKING TIME: 25 MINUTES

100g (3½oz) savoy cabbage, sliced wafer thin

3 tablespoons vegetable oil

2 garlic cloves, crushed

4cm (1½in) piece fresh ginger, finely chopped

150g (5½oz) shiitake mushrooms, finely chopped

3 spring onions (scallions), thinly sliced

3 carrots, grated

1 large bunch coriander (cilantro), finely chopped

1 teaspoon ground white pepper

1 tablespoon light soy sauce

1 teaspoon sesame oil

36 round wonton wrappers

For the dipping sauce

4 tablespoons light soy sauce

3 tablespoons black vinegar

1 teaspoon caster (superfine) sugar

2 tablespoons chilli oil

To make the dipping sauce, mix together all the ingredients.

Finely chop the cabbage slices. Place 1 tablespoon vegetable oil, the garlic and ginger in a large wok over medium heat. Cook, stirring, for 1 minute, then add the chopped cabbage, mushrooms, spring onions and carrots. Stir-fry for 5 minutes until the mixture softens and any liquid evaporates. Remove from the heat and stir in the coriander, pepper, soy sauce, sesame oil and a generous pinch of salt. Allow to cool a little.

Place 2 teaspoons of this filling in the middle of a wonton wrapper and brush the edge with water. Fold over to form a half-moon shape, pleating the edges together about five times as you go. Press the edges firmly to seal completely. Sit the dumplings so the seam is vertical and the base is flat, on a baking tray lined with baking paper. Cover with a damp tea towel as you make them.

Now, pour 1 tablespoon of the remaining oil into a large non-stick frying pan and set over a medium heat. Add half the dumplings to the pan, with the flat base down. Cook, undisturbed, for about 2 minutes until golden underneath. Pour 200ml (7floz) water into the pan, bring to the boil then reduce the heat slightly. Cover with a lid or large baking tray and simmer for about 8 minutes, or until no liquid remains in the pan. Serve straight away with half the dipping sauce and repeat the cooking process with the remaining dumplings.

For a rustic look, try crushing the coated cheese slightly with the back of a fork. Drizzle the bites with olive oil and offer toasted flatbreads to scoop them up.

Roasted red capsicum and goat's cheese bites

MAKES ABOUT 30
PREPARATION TIME: 15 MINUTES

2 roasted red capsicums (peppers) in olive oil, drained and chopped

250g (9oz) soft goat's cheese, curd cheese or labne (see page 38)

2 tablespoons coriander seeds, toasted and crushed

1 teaspoon black pepper, crushed

4 tablespoons finely chopped coriander (cilantro)

extra virgin olive oil, to cover (optional)

Stir the chopped capsicums into the cheese and roll into heaped teaspoon-sized balls.

Combine the coriander seeds, black pepper and chopped coriander with a pinch of salt and spread out on a large plate. Roll the cheese rounds in this mixture to coat.

Serve the cheese rounds as they are with crisp flatbread or, if you'd rather save them for another time, place in a bowl or jar and cover with extra virgin olive oil. Chill and eat within a couple of weeks.

Serrano chillies are the longish, pointed variety commonly available in supermarkets: use red or green in the guacamole as you wish, but go easy if they are extra fiery. This dish also works well with large potatoes.

Cumin potato skins and guacamole salsa

SERVES 4
PREPARATION TIME: 20 MINUTES
COOKING TIME: ABOUT 1 HOUR 15 MINUTES

15 new potatoes or small waxy potatoes

3 tablespoons olive oil

2 teaspoons cumin seeds

For the salsa

4 large, ripe avocados, halved, stones removed

½ teaspoon cumin seeds, lightly toasted and crushed

2 ripe tomatoes, seeded and diced

½ red onion, finely chopped

2 serrano chillies, seeded and finely chopped

juice of 1 large or 2 small limes

2 tablespoons chopped coriander (cilantro)

Preheat the oven to 180°C (350°F/Gas 4). Scrub the potatoes lightly if they look dirty, sprinkle with a little salt and bake for 50–60 minutes until tender. Set aside to cool a little. Cut each potato in half and scoop out the flesh. (The flesh is perfect for turning into mash – just beat in butter, salt and milk to taste – or vegetable patties.) Drizzle the potato skins with the olive oil and rub in the cumin seeds and a generous sprinkle of salt. Space out on a baking tray and bake for 15 minutes or so until crisp and golden.

Meanwhile, to make the salsa, roughly mash the avocados with a fork (you don't want them smooth; the aim is to leave a lot of texture). Stir in the remaining ingredients and season to taste.

Serve the crisp potato skins alongside the salsa, with a spoon for scooping, or spoon the salsa into each potato half and eat before they soften.

This recipe can be adapted for large potatoes: bake 4 potatoes for 1 hour 20 minutes then halve, scoop out the flesh and cut the skin into strips before serving with the salsa.

The salty feta is tempered with creamy fromage frais and is balanced by the honey-sweet pumpkin, while the spicy harissa paste - a hot North African chilli sauce - adds a touch of fire to these crisp tarts.

Spiced pumpkin and feta puff pastry tarts

SERVES 4
PREPARATION TIME: 20 MINUTES
COOKING TIME: 40-45 MINUTES

400g (14oz) pumpkin (squash), sliced

1 tablespoon olive oil

100g (3½oz) feta cheese

1 tablespoon harissa

1 egg, beaten

2 tablespoons fromage frais or cottage cheese

a little plain (all-purpose) flour, for dusting

375g (13oz) all-butter puff pastry

4 thyme sprigs, leaves stripped

Preheat the oven to 200°C (400°F/Gas 6). Toss the pumpkin with the olive oil, season with salt and pepper and spread out in a roasting tin. Cook for about 25 minutes until tender. Set aside to cool a little. Reduce the oven temperature to 190°C (375°F/Gas 5).

Cut half the feta into small cubes and crumble the rest. Beat the harissa, egg, fromage frais or cottage cheese and crumbled feta together in a bowl and season with pepper and just a little salt (the cheese is already salty).

Lightly flour a work surface and roll out the pastry until it's about 20 x 30cm (8 x 12in). Trim with a sharp knife so the sides are straight, and cut into 12 equal-sized rectangles. Spread out on a baking tray. Spoon a little of the harissa mixture on the centre of each piece of pastry and top with the pumpkin slices and feta cubes. Sprinkle with the thyme and bake for 15-20 minutes until puffed and golden. Serve warm, or cool the tarts on a wire rack.

This full-flavour trio is dedicated to all things mellow and earthy: roast garlic is subtle, carrots are sweet, tahini and lentils are nutty. I serve the hummus in bowls, with a pile of crisp toasts alongside.

Puy lentil hummus and carrot and cumin hummus with garlic toasts

SERVES 4
PREPARATION TIME: 20 MINUTES
COOKING TIME: I HOUR I5 MINUTES

I garlic bulb, unpeeled

olive oil, for drizzling

2 seeded bread rolls

For the lentil hummus

I75g (6oz) puy lentils or tiny blue-green lentils, rinsed and drained

4 sun-dried tomatoes in oil

2 tablespoons chopped parsley

I tablespoon lemon juice

For the carrot hummus

2 large carrots, sliced

2 tablespoons olive oil

300g (I0½oz) cooked chickpeas or 400g (I4oz) tin chickpeas, well drained

I tablespoon light tahini

a pinch of ground cardamom

I tablespoon lemon juice

Preheat the oven to 200°C (400°F/Gas 6). Slice the top off the garlic bulb to just expose the cloves. Drizzle with olive oil and wrap loosely in foil, sealing securely. Bake for 30 minutes or so until soft. When cooked, squeeze the garlic from the bulb into a bowl, mash with a fork and add a good drizzle of olive oil and a pinch of salt Cut the bread rolls into slices 5mm (¼in) thick at most, and brush both sides with the garlic mixture. Spread out on a baking tray and place in the oven for a few minutes until just turning golden at the edges.

To make the lentil hummus, cover the lentils with 500ml (I7floz) water in a saucepan and bring to the boil. Simmer gently for about 30 minutes, stirring occasionally until the liquid has been absorbed. Transfer to a blender and add I teaspoon of the garlic mixture, the sun-dried tomatoes and a drizzle of their oil, parsley and lemon juice. Blend to a rough purée, adding a little water if necessary, and season to taste with salt and pepper.

To make the carrot hummus, put the carrots in a saucepan with enough water to cover them. Add the oil and a pinch of salt and bring to the boil. Simmer for 8 minutes until the carrots are tender. Pour the whole lot into a blender with the chickpeas, tahini, cardamom, lemon juice and I teaspoon of the garlic mixture and blend to a purée. Serve with the garlic toasts and lentil hummus.

To make a fresh chutney to go with the pakoras, blend a large handful of chopped mint with a small handful of chopped coriander (cilantro). Chop a small red onion and a couple of green chillies and add them to the herbs with a squeeze of lime, a generous splash of water and a pinch of salt.

Spring vegetable pakoras

MAKES ABOUT 20
PREPARATION TIME: 20 MINUTES
COOKING TIME: 2-3 MINUTES PER BATCH

½ teaspoon cumin seeds, crushed

½ teaspoon coriander seeds, crushed

½ teaspoon ground turmeric

½ teaspoon chilli powder

½ teaspoon salt

¼ teaspoon baking powder

200g (7oz) gram or chickpea flour

1 litre (35floz) vegetable oil, for deep-frying

200g (7oz) purple sprouting broccoli or broccolini, roughly chopped

100g (3½oz) peas

5 spring onions (scallions), roughly chopped

Mix the cumin, coriander, turmeric, chilli powder, salt, baking powder and gram flour together in a large bowl and gradually whisk in 200ml (7floz) cold water to form a batter.

Heat the oil in a deep saucepan or wok until it reaches 180°C (350°F/Gas 4). If you don't have a thermometer drop a little batter into the pan – it should sizzle and dance immediately if hot enough.

Add the broccoli, peas and spring onions to the batter and stir to coat. Drop tablespoons of this mixture into the hot oil, being careful not to overcrowd the pan, and deep-fry for 2-3 minutes until golden brown. Lift out with a slotted spoon and drain on paper towel. Serve immediately, perhaps with the fresh chutney described above.

Preparing this dish is just so simple and the real bonus is that only three ingredients are needed for the terrine. It's sublime served with mayonnaise, but the terrine also works well with a basic vinaigrette.

Pressed leek terrine with dijon mayonnaise

SERVES 8
PREPARATION TIME: 20 MINUTES
PLUS PRESSING AND CHILLING TIME
COOKING TIME: 10-12 MINUTES

1.2kg (2lb1loz) young, slender leeks

½ small bunch chives, finely chopped

100g (3½oz) fromage blanc or curd cheese

For the dijon mayonnaise

4 tablespoons mayonnaise (see page 137) or good-quality bought mayonnaise

1 teaspoon dijon mustard

Line a standard terrine mould or loaf tin with plastic wrap. Trim the leeks to roughly the same length as the terrine mould, leaving a little green at the ends. Rinse them well under cold running water to wash away any grit. Drop the leeks into a large pan of salted, boiling water and simmer for 10-12 minutes until completely tender to the point of a knife. Drain and leave to cool slightly.

Sprinkle the base of the terrine mould with 1 teaspoon of the chopped chives then cover with the leeks, laying them lengthways and alternating white and green ends. Cover with a few evenly spaced teaspoonfuls of cheese. Season well with pepper, a little salt and more chopped chives. Keep layering until all the ingredients have been used, finishing with a snug layer of leeks. Cover with plastic wrap and weigh down with a couple of unopened food tins. Chill for at least 4 hours or preferably overnight.

To make the dijon mayonnaise, combine the mayonnaise and mustard in a small bowl.

Using a sharp, serrated knife, slice the terrine very carefully and transfer to serving plates. You should get at least eight slices from the terrine. Serve with the dijon mayonnaise.

This cheese looks beautiful and tastes even better. Let it marinate for at least a day before using in salads or on fresh bread. It will last in its oil for up to 2 weeks if you keep it chilled.

How to make labne

step 1

Rinse and wring out a sheet of muslin and use it to line a colander or sieve, ensuring the excess cloth overhangs the edges. Set the colander or sieve in or over a mixing bowl.

step 2

Stir ½ teaspoon salt into 500g (1lb 2oz) plain yoghurt (or 3 tablespoons caster/superfine sugar if you would prefer a sweet cheese). You can also add flavourings and spices at this stage: citrus zest, a teaspoon of crushed coriander or cumin seeds, a pinch of chilli flakes, chopped herbs or vanilla seeds that have been scraped from a vanilla bean.

step 3

Spoon the yoghurt into the cloth and fold the overhanging edges over.

Ingredients for your labne include: plain yoghurt, salt, caster (superfine) sugar, lemon, dried apricots, coriander seeds, cumin seeds, chilli flakes, thyme and other fresh herbs, olive oil.

caster sugar

unwrap

add olive oil, herbs and seeds

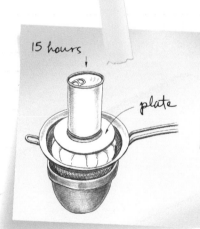

15 hours

plate

step 4

Set a small plate on top and weigh down with a can or bottle (you will not need much weight to press the yoghurt). Leave in a cool place for up to 15 hours.

step 5

The longer you leave the cheese, the firmer it will be. To speed up the process, gently squeeze the muslin to force extra water out of the cheese. Carefully unwrap and turn the cheese onto a plate. It will have a domed shape with beautiful markings from the cloth.

step 6

Use as is, or beat in herbs for a savoury version, or chopped dried fruit for a sweet cheese. The drained whey can be used to make bread. The cheese will keep, chilled and covered, for up to 4 days. You can also roll it into walnut-sized balls and keep in a sterilised jar; pour in enough extra virgin olive oil to cover and add a few robust herb stalks, such as rosemary or thyme, and perhaps a few coriander seeds. Leave the cheese to marinate for at least a day before eating in salads or on fresh bread.

This is a beautiful gossamer-fine salad, more suited to a role as a starter than a main course. It's incredibly lovely but not quite substantial enough to call itself a main meal.

Shaved salad with toasted seeds

SERVES 4
PREPARATION TIME: 25 MINUTES

2 medium beetroot with leaves, scrubbed but not peeled

2 small fennel bulbs, halved

½ young tender rhubarb stalk

I red apple, quartered and cored

2 witlof (chicory) bulbs, shredded

3 tablespoons mixed seeds, toasted

For the dressing

2 tablespoons cider vinegar

4 tablespoons extra virgin olive oil

I teaspoon fennel seeds

a small handful of fennel fronds, roughly chopped

To make the dressing, whisk all the ingredients together and season well.

Trim the leaves from the beetroot and reserve.

Use a mandolin slicer, a sharp knife or even a vegetable peeler to pare the beetroot, fennel bulbs, rhubarb and apple into fine strips or slices. Place in a bowl and add the beetroot leaves and shredded witlof. Toss with the dressing.

Divide the salad among serving plates and scatter each serving with a couple of teaspoons of toasted seeds.

Mujadhara, a traditional Middle Eastern dish, is a delicious combination of golden onions, lentils and rice. Tossed with parsley and baby spinach, it makes a lovely base for this warm salad of slow-roasted tomatoes and creamy labne.

Warm salad of slow-roasted tomatoes and labne on mujadhara

SERVES 4
PREPARATION TIME: 20 MINUTES
COOKING TIME: 1 HOUR

a pinch of saffron threads

2 tablespoons sherry vinegar

3 tablespoons olive oil

1 large bunch flat-leaf parsley, leaves only

50g (1¾oz) baby English spinach

150g (5½oz) labne (see page 38) or curd cheese

3 tablespoons flaked almonds, lightly toasted

For the slow-roasted tomato halves

1 kg (2lb4oz) ripe sweet tomatoes, halved

2 tablespoons caster (superfine) sugar

2 tablespoons chopped rosemary

3 garlic cloves, finely chopped

olive oil, for drizzling

For the mujadhara

2 tablespoons olive oil

1 large onion, sliced

250g (9oz) brown lentils

150g (5½oz) brown basmati rice

To prepare the slow-roasted tomatoes, preheat the oven to 110°C (225°F/Gas ½). Place the tomatoes on two baking trays, cut sides up. Sprinkle with the sugar, rosemary, garlic and salt and pepper. Drizzle with olive oil. Roast for about 4 hours, depending on the size of the tomatoes, until shrunken and a little blackened at the edges. If the tomatoes are very large, they can take up to 6 hours, but cherry tomatoes will take about 3 hours.

To make the mujadhara, warm the oil in a large saucepan, add the sliced onion with a generous pinch of salt and soften over a low heat for 20 minutes. Turn up the heat and fry for 10 minutes more until the onion is deeply golden. Add the brown lentils and cover with 600ml (21floz) water. Bring to the boil, cover and simmer gently for 10 minutes. Stir in the rice, cover and simmer for 20 minutes more. Remove from the heat and leave to steam for 10 minutes.

Meanwhile, soak the saffron in a couple of tablespoons of boiling water for 5 minutes. Add the vinegar and olive oil to make a dressing and season with salt and pepper.

Combine the parsley (reserving a small handful) and spinach with the mujadhara. Pile into a serving bowl and top with the tomatoes, scoops of labne or curd cheese, flaked almonds, the remaining parsley (roughly chopped) and the dressing. Serve warm or at room temperature.

This is a deeply gratifying dish for chilly months – it offers the fresh and lively flavours of a salad, but the comfort of a more substantial meal. Keep an eye on the nuts after adding them to the roast carrots and shallots – they're all too easy to scorch.

Winter salad

SERVES 4
PREPARATION TIME: 20 MINUTES
COOKING TIME: ABOUT 35 MINUTES

300g (10½oz) small carrots

6 French shallots, halved

4 tablespoons olive oil

150g (5½oz) walnuts, roughly chopped

150g (5½oz) prunes, pitted and halved

200g (7oz) faro or spelt

2 tablespoons sherry vinegar

½ garlic clove, crushed

1 teaspoon dijon mustard

1 small bunch flat-leaf parsley, leaves chopped

175g (6oz) goat's cheese

Preheat the oven to 190°C (375°F/Gas 5). Halve or thickly slice the carrots, depending on their size, and toss with the shallots, 2 tablespoons of the olive oil and plenty of salt and pepper. Spread out on a baking tray and roast for about 25 minutes until caramelised and soft. Add the walnuts and prunes to the tray, sprinkling them evenly over the vegetables, and return to the oven to toast for a further 5–10 minutes.

Meanwhile, cover the faro with 500ml (17floz) cold water in a saucepan. Add a generous pinch of salt and bring to the boil. Cover and reduce the heat, leaving the faro to simmer merrily for 25 minutes. Drain off any remaining water then cover the pan and set the faro aside.

Make the dressing by whisking the remaining olive oil, vinegar, garlic and mustard together with a little salt and pepper. The dressing should be slightly sharp to counter the sweet carrots and prunes.

Combine the faro, carrot mixture, half the parsley and half the dressing in a serving bowl. Crumble the goat's cheese over the salad, drizzle with the remaining dressing and scatter with the rest of the parsley.

This warm salad bursts with the sweet tastes of North Africa and the extra large couscous grains absorb all the delicious flavours. It's a breeze to make the chermoula dressing and this versatile seasoning is always handy to have on standby in the refrigerator.

Giant couscous salad with preserved lemon and chermoula

SERVES 4
PREPARATION TIME: 25 MINUTES
COOKING TIME: 50 MINUTES

500g (1lb2oz) young parsnips

3 red capsicums (peppers), sliced

3 tablespoons olive oil

2 tablespoons honey

2 preserved lemons, quartered

150g (5½oz) Israeli or giant couscous

1 quantity chermoula dressing (see page 141)

juice of 1 lemon

1 small bunch coriander (cilantro), leaves only

200g (7oz) Greek-style yoghurt

Preheat the oven to 200°C (400°F/Gas 6). Slice the parsnips lengthways into halves or quarters, depending on their size. Place in a roasting tin with the capsicums and coat with half the olive oil and honey. Season well and roast for 35 minutes until caramelised.

Slice the flesh from the preserved lemon quarters and discard. Cut the peel into strips and set aside.

Heat the remaining olive oil in a large saucepan, add the couscous and stir over a medium heat until golden – this will only take about 4 minutes. Pour in 200ml (7floz) boiling water and simmer gently for about 10 minutes until the water has been absorbed and the couscous is tender.

Combine the roasted vegetables with the couscous in a large serving bowl. Add 1 tablespoon of the chermoula dressing, the preserved lemon peel, lemon juice and most of the coriander.

Swirl the remaining chermoula dressing through the yoghurt and serve a spoonful on the salad, topped with the rest of the coriander.

When blood oranges come into season, celebrate them with this salad. The contrasting colours of the snow-white cheese, purple leaves and deep red fruit looks glorious, and tastes it, too. It's best eaten as fresh as possible, so make it at the very last minute.

Blood orange, mozzarella, toasted sourdough and radicchio salad

SERVES 4
PREPARATION TIME: 15 MINUTES
COOKING TIME: 15 MINUTES

3 thick slices sourdough bread

a little olive oil

3 blood oranges

2 tablespoons red wine vinegar

4 tablespoons extra virgin olive oil

1 medium head of radicchio, trimmed

a handful of wild rocket (arugula)

2 balls buffalo mozzarella, torn into pieces

Preheat the oven to 180°C (350°F/Gas 4). Roughly tear the bread into pieces – they should be about the size of a small egg – and coat with the olive oil. Spread out on a baking tray and bake for about 15 minutes, shaking and stirring halfway, until golden and crisp. Set aside.

Meanwhile, place the oranges in a shallow dish – you want to catch all the juice – and cut off the tops and bottoms to expose the flesh, then carefully pare the skin away from the sides, following the curve of the fruit. Slice horizontally into discs. Measure 4 tablespoons of the collected juice into a separate bowl, whisk in the vinegar and olive oil, and season with salt and pepper.

Tear the radicchio into large pieces and add to a large bowl with the rocket. Toss in the toasted bread, orange slices and mozzarella pieces. Drizzle with the dressing and toss very gently. Serve straight away.

Quinoa is not actually a grain, but a member of the beet and spinach family. It is, however, cooked in a very similar way to most other wholegrains. Here it is simmered to tenderness in a mushroom stock. When cooked, each grain will unfurl like a stretched coil.

Quinoa with parsley pesto, cranberries, toasted hazelnuts and mushrooms

SERVES 4
PREPARATION TIME: 25 MINUTES
COOKING TIME: 30 MINUTES

15g (½oz) dried porcini or other mushrooms

30g (1oz) butter

1 tablespoon olive oil

250g (9oz) mixed fresh mushrooms, sliced if large

2 French shallots, finely chopped

1 garlic clove, finely chopped

175g (6oz) quinoa

100g (3½oz) dried cranberries

1 quantity parsley pesto (see page 137) made with hazelnuts instead of almonds

a squeeze of lemon

75g (2½oz) hazelnuts, toasted and roughly chopped

Place the dried mushrooms in a heatproof measuring cup. Add enough just-boiled water to reach the 350ml (12floz) mark. Set aside.

Melt half the butter with the olive oil in a deep frying pan. Keep the heat high and fry the fresh mushrooms briskly for a couple of minutes, stirring until they are golden. Tip into a bowl and set aside. Return the pan to a slightly more gentle heat. Add the remaining butter and the shallots to the pan and cook for a few minutes until the shallots are softened. Add the garlic and quinoa and cook, stirring, for 5 minutes until the quinoa takes on a pale golden colour.

Strain the soaked mushrooms through a sieve, reserving the water, and roughly chop, then add them to the quinoa. Pour in the strained mushroom water and bring to the boil. Throw in a good pinch of salt, reduce the heat and simmer gently for 18-20 minutes until the quinoa is tender and the liquid is absorbed. Fold in the cranberries and reserved browned mushrooms and set aside.

Stir a couple of tablespoons of the parsley pesto through the salad, plus a squeeze of lemon juice. Spoon a little more pesto over the salad and sprinkle with the hazelnuts. Best served warm.

Cherry tomatoes come in a rainbow of colours and a range of shapes and sizes: red, orange, yellow, black, round, oval and teardrop. A selection looks stunning atop this verdant tabbouleh.

Green tabbouleh topped with a cherry tomato salad

SERVES 4
PREPARATION TIME: 15 MINUTES
PLUS SOAKING TIME

150g (5½oz) burghul (bulgur)

2 large bunches flat-leaf parsley, leaves only

1 large bunch mint, leaves only

½ cucumber, peeled, seeded and very finely diced

1 bunch spring onions (scallions), thinly sliced

juice of 2 lemons

4 tablespoons olive oil

300g (10½oz) cherry tomatoes, halved if large

Generously cover the burghul with warm water and leave to soak for 1 hour. Drain well, squeezing the excess water out.

Finely chop the parsley and mint leaves. Mix with the drained burghul, add the diced cucumber and stir well. Add most of the spring onions, reserving some for the tomato salad.

Combine the lemon juice with the olive oil and season well with salt and pepper to make a dressing. Pour most of the dressing over the tabbouleh. Taste and adjust the seasoning as needed, then spoon the tabbouleh onto a serving plate. Top with the cherry tomatoes, a scattering of the remaining spring onions and the rest of the dressing.

The contrasting toppings of this spiced, Indian-style salad sing with crisp pomegranate seeds and luscious yoghurt. Texture is just as important as wonderful flavour and vibrant colour in this dish.

Chana chaat

SERVES 4
PREPARATION TIME: 25 MINUTES
COOKING TIME: 15 MINUTES

1 small onion, halved and sliced

2cm (¾in) piece fresh ginger, finely grated

1 green chilli, seeded and finely chopped

2 tablespoons peanut oil

300g (10½oz) cooked chickpeas or 400g (14oz) tin chickpeas, drained

½ teaspoon mild chilli powder

1 teaspoon garam masala

½ cucumber, peeled, seeded and diced

2 vine-ripened tomatoes, diced

a squeeze of lemon

1 small bunch coriander (cilantro), roughly chopped, plus extra leaves to serve

2 large cooked poppadoms, roughly broken

4 heaped tablespoons plain yoghurt

seeds from 1 pomegranate

Sauté the onion, ginger and chilli in the oil for 5 minutes until the onion is soft. Add the chickpeas and cook for a further 5 minutes until golden. Now add the chilli powder and garam masala and cook for 2 minutes more. Remove from the heat, season well and set aside to cool.

Mix the cucumber, tomatoes, lemon juice and the chopped coriander in a mixing bowl. Divide among four plates and top with the broken poppadoms, chickpea mixture, yoghurt and pomegranate seeds.

Sprinkle with the coriander leaves and serve before the poppadoms soften.

Choose a really ripe camembert or brie for this salad and the most luscious black figs you can lay your hands on, and you will have the perfect partnership.

Camembert, watercress and marinated figs with walnut dressing

SERVES 4
PREPARATION TIME: 25 MINUTES
PLUS MARINATING TIME
COOKING TIME: 10 MINUTES

200ml (7floz) balsamic vinegar

100g (3½oz) caster (superfine) sugar

2 garlic cloves, bruised

6 thyme sprigs

6 plump figs, halved lengthways

4 tablespoons walnut oil

a large handful of watercress, thick stalks trimmed

150g (5½oz) ripe camembert or brie, sliced

75g (2½oz) walnuts, toasted and roughly chopped

Place the vinegar, sugar, garlic and 4 of the thyme sprigs in a saucepan and add 100ml (3½floz) water. Bring to the boil and simmer for 1 minute to dissolve the sugar and cook out some of the vinegary flavour. Set aside to cool for 5 minutes, then pour over the halved figs and leave to marinate for an hour or two.

Discard the thyme sprigs and garlic from the marinade and spoon 5 tablespoons into a small lidded jar. Strip the leaves from the remaining 2 thyme sprigs and add to the jar with the walnut oil, a little salt and plenty of pepper. Screw on the lid and shake well until combined to make a dressing.

Heat a non-stick frying pan over a medium-high heat and sear the drained figs, cut sides down, for a minute or so until they caramelise. Remove the pan from the heat, turn the figs over and set aside.

Put the watercress in a large bowl and drizzle with a little of the dressing, tossing to coat the leaves. Add the camembert or brie, walnuts and figs and divide among serving plates. Spoon the remaining dressing over each plate of salad.

Salad toppings

Toasted garlic breadcrumbs

Warm about 3 tablespoons fruity olive oil in a large frying pan with 2 crushed garlic cloves and cook over a very low heat for a few minutes. Add a cupful of stale breadcrumbs made from ciabatta or sourdough. Stir over a medium heat for a few minutes until the crumbs are browned and toasted, then set aside to cool.

Maple walnuts

Coat 100g (3½oz) walnut halves with 2 tablespoons maple syrup, 1 tablespoon finely chopped rosemary and a pinch of cayenne pepper. Season well. Spread on a baking tray lined with baking paper and bake at 160°C (315°F/Gas 2-3) for 15 minutes, stirring halfway, until golden. Set aside to cool before roughly chopping.

Tahini seeds

Spread 200g (7oz) mixed seeds on a large baking tray and roast at 180°C (350°F/Gas 4) for 5 minutes. Combine 2 tablespoons light tahini, 1 tablespoon honey, 1 tablespoon sesame oil and ½ a crushed garlic clove in a large bowl. Tip in the hot seeds and mix well. Spread out on the baking tray again and bake for another 5 minutes. Set aside to cool, then crumble over salads as needed.

Olive and polenta cubes

Stir 250g (9oz) quick-cook polenta in 1 litre (35floz) simmering vegetable stock for 3 minutes until thick. Stir in 1 large handful grated parmesan cheese and 4 tablespoons finely chopped olives. Season well. Spread out on a tray to a thickness of about 2.5cm (1in) and cool. Once firm, cut the polenta into 2.5cm (1in) cubes and sauté in olive oil until browned.

Roasted spiced chickpeas

Thoroughly drain 800g (1lb12oz) freshly cooked or tinned chickpeas, then toss with 1 tablespoon olive oil, 1 teaspoon ground coriander, 1 teaspoon ground cumin and a pinch of cayenne pepper. Spread on a baking tray lined with baking paper. Cook for about 45 minutes at 180°C (350°F/Gas 4) until crisp and golden, shaking the tray every now and then.

Crisp parmesan lace

Line a large baking tray with baking paper. Drop mounds of finely grated parmesan cheese onto the tray at regular intervals (it will spread out as it cooks) and bake at 200°C (400°F/Gas 6) for 3-4 minutes until golden and bubbling. Leave to settle for a minute, then remove with a spatula and leave to cool. Scatter over salads as they are, or break into pieces.

This is for days when you can't bring yourself to switch on the oven or stove, because there's no cooking involved at all. It's a very satisfying dish, as the ripe avocado adds body and richness to all that raw vegetable virtue.

Raw vegetable and avocado soup

SERVES 4
PREPARATION TIME: 10 MINUTES

3 large carrots

50g (1¾oz) English spinach leaves

4 celery stalks

3cm (1in) piece fresh ginger

2 large, very ripe avocados, halved, stones removed

iced water

juice of ½ lime

1 tablespoon soy sauce

2–3 drops Tabasco sauce

ice cubes, toasted sesame oil and coriander (cilantro) leaves, to serve

Pass the carrots, spinach, celery and ginger through a juicer and then transfer the juice to a blender. Blitz with the avocados until smooth. Make the quantity up to 800ml (28floz) with iced water, lime juice, soy sauce and Tabasco sauce. Blend again.

Serve the soup with ice cubes, a drop or two of sesame oil and some coriander leaves.

This soup should taste of sunshine, so you'll need the ripest and freshest vegetables you can find to do it justice. If you want to gild the lily further, some good black olives, pitted and diced, and a few oregano leaves are lovely when added to the vegetable garnish.

Gazpacho

SERVES 4
PREPARATION TIME: 20 MINUTES
TIME

700g (1lb9oz) vine-ripened tomatoes

2 red capsicums (peppers), halved and seeded

1 large cucumber

1 garlic clove, crushed

½ loaf ciabatta, torn

4 tablespoons sherry vinegar

100ml (3½floz) extra virgin olive oil

2 teaspoons caster (superfine) sugar

Tabasco sauce, to serve (optional)

ice cubes and basil leaves, to serve

Set aside 2 tomatoes, half a red capsicum and a quarter of the cucumber.

Roughly chop the remaining tomatoes, capsicums and cucumber and place in a blender with the garlic and bread. Blend to a rough purée, then transfer to a bowl and stir in the vinegar and 200ml (7floz) water. Season with salt and pepper. Cover and chill for at least 2 hours or overnight. The bread will swell up and the flavours will mellow.

Before serving, nick the bases of the reserved tomatoes, place in a heatproof bowl and cover with boiling water. Drain the tomatoes and peel the skin away. Chop into fine dice, along with the reserved red capsicum and cucumber.

Stir the olive oil into the gazpacho and taste again. Add the sugar, Tabasco sauce (if using) or a little more vinegar, salt or pepper, and even a little extra chilled water to adjust the consistency. The soup should have quite a kick to it so make sure it's nice and punchy.

Divide the soup among chilled bowls and serve with the ice cubes, a scattering of the diced vegetables and basil leaves.

There might be a lot of chopping here, but this recipe is child's play and the result is special enough to warrant the extra effort. The cream adds a certain silky richness but can be left out if you prefer. This is lovely served cool the next day.

Summer minestrone

SERVES 4
PREPARATION TIME: 15 MINUTES
COOKING TIME: 45 MINUTES

2 tablespoons olive oil

2 garlic cloves, finely chopped

2 French shallots, finely chopped

2 celery stalks, finely chopped

1 fennel bulb, finely chopped

200g (7oz) young broad beans, podded weight, skins removed

200g (7oz) young fresh peas

150g (5½oz) green beans, sliced

250g (9oz) asparagus spears, sliced

950ml (33floz) vegetable stock (see page 136) or good-quality bought stock

a handful each of mint and basil leaves

4 tablespoons thick (double) cream

4 tablespoons fresh pesto (see page 137), to serve

Heat the olive oil in a large saucepan and soften the garlic, shallots, celery and fennel. It should take about 10 minutes.

Add half the broad beans, peas, green beans and asparagus. Cook, stirring, for 5 minutes. Pour in the stock, bring to the boil and simmer for about 25 minutes.

Add the remaining vegetables to the saucepan and cook for 5 minutes more. Remove from the heat and pour in a little extra boiling water if the soup appears too thick for your liking. Add the herbs and cream and season to taste.

Ladle the soup into warmed bowls and drop a spoonful of pesto into each to serve.

The humble potato has been ruthlessly fired from chowder duty and replaced with the more vivacious butternut pumpkin. Don't hesitate to reinstate potato if you have some to hand – 500g (1lb2oz) will do nicely – to produce a slightly milder soup.

Pumpkin and corn chowder

SERVES 4
PREPARATION TIME: 20 MINUTES
COOKING TIME: 30 MINUTES

1 small butternut pumpkin (squash)

40g (1½oz) butter

1 small onion, finely chopped

1 fennel bulb, finely chopped

1 carrot, finely chopped

1 garlic clove, finely chopped

½ teaspoon chilli flakes

2 tablespoons plain (all-purpose) flour

700ml (24floz) vegetable stock (see page 136) or good-quality bought stock

200ml (7floz) milk

2 corn cobs, kernels sliced off

a small bunch of dill, finely chopped

a squeeze of lime, to taste

Cut the pumpkin in half lengthways and scoop out the seeds. Peel and chop the flesh into large cubes.

Melt the butter in a large, deep saucepan. Add the chopped onion, fennel, carrot and garlic, and cook gently for 10 minutes, stirring often, until softened but not coloured. Add the chilli flakes and flour and stir for 1 minute, then add the pumpkin and stock. Bring to the boil, then reduce the heat and simmer for 10 minutes until the pumpkin is tender.

Add the milk, corn and dill and simmer for 5 minutes more. Season well and add a squeeze of lime.

Sometimes a rich main course demands a light starter, and this fits the bill very prettily: a ruby broth that will tempt but not overfill diners. Do try to avoid the beetroot that's ready-cooked, vinegared and wrapped in plastic – you want the fresh stuff full of all that sweet, earthy flavour.

Beetroot and porcini broth

SERVES 4
PREPARATION TIME: 10 MINUTES
COOKING TIME: 30 MINUTES
PLUS STEEPING TIME

3 large beetroot, peeled and roughly chopped

2 carrots, roughly chopped

1 celery stalk, roughly chopped

20g (¾oz) dried porcini mushrooms

a handful of chervil or flat-leaf parsley including stalks, plus extra sprigs to garnish

a squeeze of lemon, to taste

1 teaspoon caster (superfine) sugar

Put the beetroot, carrots, celery, porcini mushrooms and chervil in a large saucepan and add 800ml (28floz) water. Bring to the boil very slowly, then reduce the heat and simmer gently for 30 minutes. Remove the pan from the heat. Leave to stand for 20 minutes, then strain the broth through a fine sieve, reserving the mushrooms and a third of the beetroot.

Finely dice the porcini and the reserved beetroot and add to the strained broth. Season with the lemon juice, sugar and some salt and pepper.

Divide the soup among serving bowls and garnish with the chervil sprigs.

Celeriac soup is heavenly and benefits from being made in advance – perhaps the night before you plan to eat it – to give the flavours time to meld. The soup will then be ready to be reheated and served hot. It is also lovely when served chilled.

Butterbean and celeriac velouté with chermoula

SERVES 4
PREPARATION TIME: 20 MINUTES
COOKING TIME: 35 MINUTES

1 celeriac, about 500g (1lb2oz), cubed

a squeeze of lemon

2 tablespoons olive oil

2 celery stalks, finely chopped

1 onion, finely chopped

2 garlic cloves, chopped

300g (10½oz) cooked butterbeans

½ teaspoon salt

2 tablespoons crème fraîche (optional)

4 tablespoons chermoula dressing (see page 141)

Drop the cubed celeriac into a bowl of cold water with a squeeze of lemon. This will stop it browning.

Heat the olive oil in a large saucepan. Add the celery, onion and garlic and cook for 10 minutes until soft and translucent but not brown. Add the drained celeriac cubes and cook for a further 5 minutes, then tip in the butterbeans with 800ml (28floz) water and the salt. Bring to the boil, then reduce the heat and simmer for about 20 minutes.

Allow the soup to cool slightly, then transfer to a blender. Blend with the crème fraîche (if using) until very smooth. For a truly velvety soup, push the mixture through a sieve. Adjust the seasoning. Serve chilled or reheat gently until piping hot. Add a spoonful of the chermoula dressing to each serving.

You can use all plain white flour in this recipe to make it a bit more refined, or half rye or spelt flour to increase the nutty overtones. The dough might seem sticky and shaggy at first, but don't worry - it's meant to look that way. And remember that a light hand really does produce a light soda bread.

Quick soda bread

MAKES 1 LARGE LOAF
PREPARATION TIME: 15 MINUTES
COOKING TIME: 45 MINUTES

250g (9oz) plain (all-purpose) flour

250g (9oz) wholemeal plain (whole-wheat all-purpose) flour

1 tablespoon caster (superfine) sugar

1 teaspoon bicarbonate of soda (baking soda)

1 teaspoon salt

30g (1oz) chilled butter, cubed

650ml (22½floz) buttermilk

Preheat the oven to 200°C (400°F/Gas 6) and line a baking tray with baking paper.

Sift the flours into a mixing bowl, adding all the bran you catch in the sieve except for 1 tablespoon, which you need to reserve for later. Stir in the sugar, bicarbonate of soda and salt. Rub in the butter with your fingertips.

Quickly stir in the buttermilk and mix with a palette knife to form a rough dough. Don't overwork the mixture or it will be tough, and work quickly as you form the dough into a round loaf. Sit the dough on the baking tray and make a deep cross in the top with a sharp knife. Sprinkle with the reserved tablespoon of bran and bake for about 45 minutes until golden and hollow-sounding when tapped underneath.

Cool the bread on a wire rack, covering with a clean tea towel if you prefer the crust to soften slightly.

Let no-one tell you that making your own bread requires some kind of talent or special culinary gift. With just a little patience (the resting time is long, but it gives this bread its lovely flavour), a chewy and tasty sourdough will be yours with barely any kneading.

No-knead sourdough loaf

MAKES 1 LOAF
PREPARATION TIME: 15 MINUTES
PLUS RESTING TIME
COOKING TIME: ABOUT 45 MINUTES

250g (9oz) strong wholemeal (whole-wheat) bread flour, plus extra for dusting

250g (9oz) strong white bread flour

¼ teaspoon instant dried yeast

1½ teaspoons salt

375ml (13floz) warm water

sunflower oil, for oiling

Combine all the dry ingredients in a large bowl and add the water, stirring with a wooden spoon and then with your hands, to form a very soft, sticky dough. It will look 'shaggy' but you don't need to over-mix it. Cover the bowl with plastic wrap and leave in a warm place for 15–18 hours.

Lightly flour a work surface and flour your hands – just a little is needed. Fold the dough over on itself, cover with oiled plastic wrap and leave for 15 minutes.

Again using minimal flour on your hands and work surface, shape the dough into a ball and slide it onto a sheet of baking paper sprinkled with wholemeal flour. Cover with a clean tea towel and leave for 2 hours until doubled in size.

Before the dough has finished rising, place a large, lidded casserole in the oven and preheat to 220°C (425°F/Gas 7). When the oven is ready, carefully take the hot casserole out, place the dough inside, and replace the lid. Return to the oven for 30 minutes, then remove the lid and cook for a further 15 minutes or so until the bread is golden on top. Tip out of the casserole and cool on a wire rack.

Think of this as an extraordinary flatbread rather than a pizza. It's rolled out slightly thicker than a conventional pizza dough and is soft and airy in the middle. Don't be fooled by the simple ingredients: it's a heavenly combination and, served straight from the oven, is beautiful with soups, salads and dips.

Pizza bianca

MAKES 4
PREPARATION TIME: 15 MINUTES
PLUS RESTING TIME
COOKING TIME: 5-10 MINUTES PER PIZZA

250g (9oz) plain (all-purpose) flour, plus extra for dusting

250g (9oz) strong white bread flour

1 teaspoon instant dried yeast

2 teaspoons salt

320ml (11floz) warm water

4 tablespoons extra virgin olive oil

polenta (cornmeal), for dusting

rosemary leaves and sea salt, to sprinkle

Combine the flours, yeast, salt and warm water in the bowl of an electric mixer or a mixing bowl to form a dough. Add 1 tablespoon of the olive oil. Using a dough hook, knead for 5-8 minutes, or turn onto a lightly floured surface and knead by hand for 10 minutes until the dough is smooth and elastic. Place in an oiled bowl, cover with plastic wrap and leave to rest in a warm place for 1 hour.

Preheat the oven to 230°C (450°F/Gas 8). If you own a pizza stone or heatproof tile that will fit inside the oven, now is the time to put it in to heat up.

Knock back the dough with a punch. Roll out a quarter of the dough on a lightly floured surface until it forms a circle about 1cm (½in) thick. Dust a baking tray with polenta and lay the pizza on it. Drizzle with olive oil and sprinkle with rosemary and sea salt. Carefully put the tray in the oven - onto the hot pizza stone or tile, if using - and cook for a few minutes. The timing will very much depend on your oven but it shouldn't be more than 8-10 minutes. While the pizza is cooking, prepare the next pizza and bake each one in quick succession. Serve each cooked pizza hot and straight out of the oven.

Like the soda bread on page 72, this recipe is quick, so you won't find any yeast here. It's an ideal mixture to experiment with: you can bake it as a whole loaf or vary the herbs and the root vegetables as you wish. This bread is forgiving and versatile but is always best served warm, preferably with a bowl of hot soup.

Parsnip and rosemary rolls

MAKES 6
PREPARATION TIME: 15 MINUTES
COOKING TIME: 25-30 MINUTES

olive oil, for oiling and drizzling

220g (7¾oz) parsnips, coarsely grated

275g (9¾oz) self-raising flour

1 tablespoon chopped rosemary, plus extra sprigs

1 teaspoon salt

2 eggs, beaten

2 tablespoons milk

Preheat the oven to 190°C (375°F/Gas 5). Oil a baking tray or line it with baking paper.

Mix the parsnips, flour, rosemary and salt in a large bowl and make a well in the centre. Add the beaten eggs and milk, then use a knife to quickly mix everything together to form a rough dough, being careful not to overwork it. Divide the dough into six pieces and shape each piece into a round. Slash the tops with a sharp knife and press a small sprig of rosemary onto each one. Drizzle with olive oil.

Bake the rolls for about 25–30 minutes until golden. Cool on a wire rack if you like, but these rolls are best eaten warm.

This makes a complete supper; it's well-balanced and quick, quick, quick. Tempeh is tofu's often overlooked cousin, made from fermented soya beans. Alternatively, you could use firm tofu here instead, and the Indian cottage cheese, paneer, would work too.

Tamarind tempeh with sesame noodles and shredded greens

SERVES 2
PREPARATION TIME: 15 MINUTES
PLUS MARINATING TIME
COOKING TIME: 10 MINUTES

250g (9oz) tempeh, sliced 2cm (¾in) thick

4cm (1½in) piece fresh ginger, finely chopped

finely grated zest and juice of 1 small orange

2 tablespoons mild honey

2 tablespoons tamarind paste or purée

2 tablespoons soy sauce, plus extra to serve

125g (4½oz) medium egg noodles

a little toasted sesame oil

2 tablespoons peanut oil

1 green chilli, seeded and finely chopped

1 garlic clove, finely chopped

150g (5½oz) Asian greens, shredded

2 teaspoons gomashio (see page 136)

2 spring onions (scallions), thinly sliced

Coat the sliced tempeh with a mixture of half the chopped ginger, the orange zest, honey, tamarind and 1 tablespoon soy sauce. Ideally, leave to marinate for 10–30 minutes.

Cook the noodles according to the packet instructions, then refresh under cold water and drain. Toss with a little sesame oil to prevent sticking and set aside.

Heat 1 tablespoon of the peanut oil in a large wok or frying pan. When the oil is almost smoking, add the tempeh and stir-fry for a few minutes, or until browned on all sides. Transfer to a plate.

Pour the remaining 1 tablespoon peanut oil into the wok and add the remaining ginger with the chilli and garlic. Cook, stirring, for 1 minute, then add the shredded greens. Return the tempeh to the wok and add the orange juice, then toss over the heat until the greens wilt. Add the drained noodles and toss to combine.

Divide the mixture between two warmed bowls and dot with a few drops of sesame oil. Sprinkle with gomashio and finish with the spring onions. Offer more soy sauce at the table.

These eggplants are a light and summery dinner option when you'd rather not spend much time in the kitchen. Make sure they are cooked to buttery tenderness before covering with the miso mixture. If you love the taste of sesame, include a few drops of sesame oil in the miso topping.

Japanese eggplant with miso

SERVES 4
PREPARATION TIME: 15 MINUTES
COOKING TIME: 6-8 MINUTES

2 tablespoons white miso paste

2 tablespoons caster (superfine) sugar

1 tablespoon mirin

1 tablespoon rice wine vinegar

4 Japanese or baby eggplants (aubergines)

2 tablespoons peanut oil

2 spring onions (scallions), finely shredded

2 tablespoons cress, ideally shiso or coriander (cilantro)

2 teaspoons sesame seeds, lightly toasted

steamed rice and pickled ginger, to serve

Combine the miso, sugar, mirin and rice wine vinegar, stirring until smooth.

Cut the eggplants into 3cm (1¼in) thick slices and brush with peanut oil on both sides. Preheat the grill (broiler) to medium and arrange the eggplant slices on a baking sheet in a single layer. Cook, positioned away from the grill, for 2 minutes on one side, then turn and cook for another couple of minutes until golden and cooked through.

Smear a little of the miso topping over each of the eggplant slices and pop them under the grill for a further 2 minutes or so. You want the topping to be caramelised and bubbling.

Scatter the grilled eggplants with shredded spring onions, cress and sesame seeds, and serve with steamed rice and pickled ginger.

If you've fallen into the habit of always boiling or steaming cauliflower, try this idea. It takes mere minutes of pan-frying, and the humble cauliflower's best nutty, sweet notes are magically unlocked. It may seem simple, but its depth of flavour justifies its place as a stand-alone meal.

Charred baby cauliflower with cumin, chilli and almonds

SERVES 4
PREPARATION TIME: 10 MINUTES
COOKING TIME: 10 MINUTES

3 tablespoons olive oil

4 baby cauliflowers, separated into small florets

1½ teaspoons cumin seeds

2 garlic cloves, thinly sliced

1 red chilli, seeded and thinly sliced

100g (3½oz) flaked almonds

1 tablespoon extra virgin olive oil

2 tablespoons chopped flat-leaf parsley

Heat the olive oil in a large wok or deep frying pan. Add the cauliflower, frying until darkly golden at the edges. Reduce the heat, cover with a lid or a baking sheet and cook for 1-2 minutes.

Add the cumin seeds, garlic, chilli and almonds. Stir-fry for 5 minutes over a medium heat until the almonds are golden. Season generously with salt and pepper, drizzle with the extra virgin olive oil and scatter with parsley.

Perfectly cooked tofu will absorb very little oil so that it emerges from the pan golden, crisp and light. The trick is to press the tofu and dry it very thoroughly before cooking it briefly. Keep your oil hot and place the cooked tofu on paper towel when it's done.

Crispy five-spice tofu with soy dipping sauce

SERVES 4
PREPARATION TIME: 20 MINUTES
COOKING TIME: 10 MINUTES

500g (1lb2oz) firm tofu

60g (2¼oz) cornflour (cornstarch)

2 tablespoons Chinese five-spice

1 teaspoon chilli flakes

100ml (3½floz) peanut oil

For the soy dipping sauce

4 tablespoons soy sauce

2 tablespoons rice wine vinegar

1 teaspoon toasted sesame oil

2cm (¾in) piece fresh ginger, very finely chopped

1 teaspoon caster (superfine) sugar

Put the tofu on a plate lined with a double layer of paper towel. Cover with another double layer of paper towel, followed by a plate, and press down firmly. Weigh the plate down with a couple of unopened tins and set aside while you prepare the rest of the recipe. Turn the oven on to a very low setting - you only need to keep the cooked tofu warm.

To make the soy dipping sauce, combine all the ingredients in a bowl, stirring to dissolve the sugar.

Combine the cornflour, five-spice and chilli flakes on a plate and spread out evenly. Measure half the oil into a large, stable wok and set over a low-medium heat. Pat the tofu dry with more paper towel and cut into large cubes. Roll the cubes in the cornflour mixture until well coated on all sides. Turn up the heat under the wok and fry half the tofu cubes, turning carefully with tongs, until crisp and golden on all sides. This will take about 5 minutes. Transfer the cooked tofu to a plate lined with paper towel to soak up excess oil and place in the oven to keep warm. Repeat with the remaining oil and tofu, then serve immediately with the dipping sauce alongside.

Protein-rich tofu has a mild and delicate flavour, making it the ideal carrier for other tastes like sesame, soy, chilli, ginger and garlic. Depending on how firm your tofu is, you can slice it and add it to salads and stir-fries.

How to make tofu

nigari + H₂O

70°C – 80°C

tofu curds

step 1

Pour 500ml (17floz) unsweetened soy milk into a pan and boil for about 5 minutes. Stand a liquid thermometer in the pan and allow the milk to cool to between 70°C and 80°C (160°F and 175°F).

step 2

Dissolve 2 teaspoons of powdered nigari in 100ml (3½floz) lukewarm water and gradually add to the soy milk, stirring constantly. If you can't find nigari, use 50ml (1½floz) white wine vinegar or lemon juice and no water. The soy milk will begin to separate and curdle and look like curds and whey.

step 3

Remove from the heat and leave for 15 minutes. Large curds should have formed, but if they look small, stir in another teaspoon of dissolved nigari. Ladle out some of the liquid tofu whey and discard. Line a colander with two layers of damp muslin and stand it over a large bowl to catch any liquid. Carefully ladle the solid tofu curds into the colander.

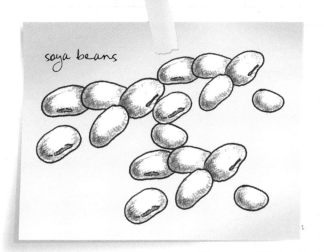

soya beans

Soy milk, made from soya beans, forms the basis of tofu. Nigari (magnesium chloride) is a tofu coagulator that causes the soy milk to separate into curds and whey, rather like the process in cheese making. Powdered nigari can be found in Japanese grocery stores or supermarkets, but you can substitute white wine vinegar or lemon juice, adding extra as needed until the soy milk curdles.

20 minutes

press

step 4

Sit a small plate on top, weigh it down with unopened tins and leave for 20 minutes to firm up.

tofu

water

step 5

Carefully unmould the drained tofu into a bowl of cold water to remove any bitterness. Soak for 10 minutes, then refresh with new water and leave to soak for a further 10 minutes.

cold water

step 6

Use the tofu straight away or gently transfer it to a lidded container, cover with cold water and refrigerate for up to 3 days.

Rigatoni is a ridged, tube-shaped pasta that goes perfectly with this comforting walnut sauce. It's not chilli hot, merely warm and toasty, making it the perfect fast food for a crisp autumn night. Serve the pasta with a pile of buttery spinach on the side if you wish.

Chilli and crushed walnut rigatoni

SERVES 4
PREPARATION TIME: 15 MINUTES
COOKING TIME: 15 MINUTES

300g (10½oz) walnut halves

1 tablespoon extra virgin olive oil

1 red chilli, seeded and finely chopped

½ garlic clove, crushed

1 teaspoon thyme leaves

2 heaped tablespoons mascarpone cheese

2 tablespoons finely grated parmesan cheese

350g (12oz) dried rigatoni pasta or similar short pasta shapes

Toast the walnuts in a dry frying pan, tossing often until golden and fragrant. Tip onto a chopping board and, when cool enough, roughly chop. Some nuts should be very fine, and some larger.

Place the olive oil, chilli and garlic in a cold frying pan and heat gently so the garlic doesn't colour. After 1–2 minutes, remove the pan from the heat. Stir in the thyme, followed by the mascarpone and parmesan. Season with salt and pepper. Stir in nearly all the walnuts, reserving a couple of tablespoons, and set aside.

Cook the pasta until al dente in a pan of salted, boiling water according to the packet instructions. Drain in a colander, reserving a few tablespoons of cooking water, and immediately return the pasta to the pan with the reserved water. Add the walnut sauce and toss through the pasta. Serve with the reserved walnuts sprinkled over the top.

The little ear shapes of orecchiette collect robust sauces better than any other pasta shape, but any small shell-like variety will work well. Don't be scared of cooking the broccoli until truly soft - this is not a dish that requires al dente vegetables.

Orecchiette with broccoli and pine nuts

SERVES 4
PREPARATION TIME: 15 MINUTES
COOKING TIME: 15 MINUTES

200g (7oz) purple sprouting broccoli or broccolini, roughly chopped

350g (12oz) dried orecchiette pasta

4 tablespoons extra virgin olive oil

1 red chilli, seeded and finely chopped

2 large garlic cloves, thinly sliced

75g (2½oz) pine nuts, toasted until golden

2 tablespoons finely grated pecorino cheese

Blanch the broccoli in plenty of boiling water for 3 minutes or so. Drain in a colander and refresh under cold running water. Drain again and roughly chop.

Cook the orecchiette until al dente in plenty of salted boiling water according to the packet instructions.

Meanwhile, combine the olive oil, chilli and sliced garlic in a cold frying pan, place over a medium heat and cook until the garlic is fragrant but not browned. Add the chopped broccoli, cover with a lid or baking sheet and cook very gently for a few minutes. Season well with salt and pepper and stir in the pine nuts.

Drain the pasta, reserving a couple of tablespoons of the cooking water. Tip the pasta into the broccoli mixture and add the pecorino and reserved cooking water. Mix well and serve.

These crisp and tender potato cakes are divine served with softly poached eggs and a punchy salsa verde. The trick to neat poached eggs is to use the freshest eggs you can find. If you make the potato cakes a few hours ahead, cooking them will be a breeze.

Potato cakes with olives and poached eggs

SERVES 4
PREPARATION TIME: 10 MINUTES
PLUS COOLING AND CHILLING TIME
COOKING TIME: 25 MINUTES

500g (1lb2oz) small waxy potatoes, such as charlotte or pink fir apple

2 French shallots, very finely chopped

2 tablespoons black olives, pitted and roughly chopped

1 tablespoon chopped flat-leaf parsley

50g (1¾oz) pecorino cheese, shaved

5 very fresh eggs

1 heaped tablespoon potato flour or plain (all-purpose) flour, plus extra for dusting

3-4 tablespoons olive oil

4 tablespoons salsa verde dressing (see page 140)

Scrub the potatoes and boil in their skins in salted water for 15 minutes, or until just tender. Drain, allow to cool for 15 minutes and then crush roughly with a fork. Add the shallots, olives, parsley and half the pecorino. Season generously with freshly ground black pepper and a little salt, and taste the mixture to make sure the seasoning is balanced. Beat 1 egg and mix into the potatoes along with the flour. Form the mixture into eight flat cakes using floured hands.

Space the potato cakes out on a plate and chill for at least 1 hour or overnight. Before cooking, generously brush the potato cakes with olive oil on both sides. Heat a large frying pan and slowly brown the potato cakes for about 4 minutes on each side, in batches if necessary. Keep warm while you poach the eggs.

Heat a deep frying pan of water until it just reaches boiling point, then reduce the heat so the base is covered in tiny bubbles. Carefully crack in the eggs, one by one, as gently as you can. Poach the eggs for 3 minutes until the whites are just set, then remove with a slotted spoon and drain on paper towel.

Place two potato cakes on each serving plate and slide a poached egg on top. Spoon the salsa verde over the egg and sprinkle with pecorino shavings.

Although fried rice is pretty quick to make, you need to start the day before, as using cooked, chilled rice is essential to get the right texture. You can use left-over rice from another dish, but ensure it's no more than a day old, and was chilled within an hour of cooking. Once the rice is done, the rest is easy.

Cashew fried rice

SERVES 4
PREPARATION TIME: 10 MINUTES
PLUS CHILLING TIME
COOKING TIME: 25 MINUTES

500g (1lb2oz) cold, cooked jasmine or basmati rice, or 240g (8½oz) uncooked rice

400g (14oz) mixed vegetables, such as snow peas (mangetout), sugar snap peas, baby corn, peas

2 tablespoons peanut oil

100g (3½oz) cashews

2 garlic cloves, finely chopped

4cm (1½in) piece fresh ginger, finely chopped

2 eggs, beaten

1 teaspoon toasted sesame oil

1-2 tablespoons soy sauce

bottled tomato chilli jam, to serve (optional)

If using the uncooked rice, start the day before. Rinse the rice well in a sieve under cold running water, then place in a saucepan. Add enough cold water to cover the rice by about 2cm (¾in). Bring to the boil, then reduce the heat and simmer for 10 minutes until all the water is absorbed. Cover the pan, remove from the heat and set aside for the rice to steam for 10 minutes. Fluff the rice up with a fork and as soon as it's cool, cover with plastic wrap and chill overnight.

When you're ready to fry the rice, blanch the vegetables in boiling water for 2 minutes. Drain in a colander and refresh under cold running water.

Heat the oil in a wok, add the cashews and stir-fry until golden. Transfer to a bowl with a slotted spoon.

Add the garlic and ginger to the wok and cook for 1 minute, then add the cold rice and vegetables, and stir-fry for a good 2 minutes to heat through. Push everything to the side of the pan and tip in the egg and sesame oil, stirring occasionally to form a sort of omelette. Break the omelette into pieces with the spatula and mix into the rice, then add the cashews.

Season the rice with soy sauce and serve with the tomato chilli jam (if using).

Tomatoes

Simple salad

Halve or slice a plateful of tomato varieties, depending on their size, and spread out on a serving plate. Whisk 50ml (1½floz) thin (pouring) cream into 50ml (1½floz) olive oil with 2 tablespoons white wine vinegar, a pinch each of caster (superfine) sugar and salt, and plenty of cracked black pepper. Drizzle over the tomatoes and scatter with fresh mint leaves.

Panzanella burrata

Roughly tear 150g (5½oz) sourdough bread into chunks and toast in the oven. Mix with 3 roughly diced vine-ripened tomatoes. Dress with some extra virgin olive oil, red wine vinegar, salt, pepper and fresh basil. Rest at room temperature for 1-2 hours. Mix in half a small, finely chopped onion and serve spooned over a ball of burrata cheese or buffalo mozzarella.

Shopska salad

Core and dice 4 large tomatoes, chop 2 seeded red capsicums (peppers) and dice 15cm (6in) of peeled and seeded cucumber. Thinly slice ½ small red onion, and finely chop 2 tablespoons flat-leaf parsley. Combine the tomatoes, capsicum, cucumber, red onion and parsley and dress with red wine vinegar, mild olive oil, salt and pepper. Coarsely grate 100g (3½oz) feta cheese over the top before serving.

Tomato and tarragon tart

Preheat the oven to 180°C (350°F/ Gas 4). Line a 12 x 35cm (4½ x 14in) tart tin with shortcrust pastry, line with baking paper and baking beans and bake for 15 minutes. Remove the beans and paper. Whisk 3 eggs with 190ml (6½floz) thin (pouring) cream and 1 tablespoon chopped tarragon. Season well. Stir in 3 peeled, seeded and sliced tomatoes. Spoon into the pastry case and bake for 25 minutes, or until just set.

Tomato and spinach dhal

Bring 250g (9oz) rinsed red lentils and 900ml (31floz) water to the boil in a large saucepan and simmer for 10 minutes. Add 400g (14oz) tin roma (plum) tomatoes, ½ teaspoon ground turmeric, 4cm (1½in) grated piece fresh ginger, 2 crushed garlic cloves, 1 teaspoon cumin seeds and 2 chopped green chillies. Stir, then simmer gently for 15–20 minutes, stirring often. Fold in 200g (7oz) baby English spinach, a squeeze of lime juice and season with salt and pepper. Eat warm with steamed rice or Indian flatbread.

Cherry tomato tarte tatin

Preheat the oven to 190°C (375°F/ Gas 5). Place a 15cm (6in) ovenproof frying pan over a low heat and add 2 tablespoons olive oil, 90g (3¼oz) golden caster (superfine) sugar and 250g (9oz) whole cherry tomatoes. Cook until the sugar caramelises to a deep golden colour, then sprinkle with 2 tablespoons balsamic vinegar. Remove from the heat and season. Tuck an 18cm (7in) circle of puff pastry over and around the tomatoes and bake for 15 minutes until the pastry is cooked. Carefully turn out onto a plate while still warm and serve with spoonfuls of the walnut tarator on page 139.

These light and fluffy little parcels don't have to be baked – you could serve them straight away with the melted herb butter or perhaps the gorgonzola sauce on page 138. It's very important to drain the ricotta thoroughly, so try to do this the day before you need it. Serve with a simple green salad.

Ricotta gnocchi gratin with parsley butter

SERVES 4
PREPARATION TIME: 30 MINUTES
PLUS DRAINING TIME
COOKING TIME: 15-20 MINUTES

450g (1lb) ricotta cheese

2 eggs, beaten

15g (½oz) butter, melted

a few gratings of nutmeg

40g (1½oz) parmesan cheese, finely grated

about 100g (3½oz) plain (all-purpose) flour, plus extra for dusting

100g (3½oz) parsley butter (see page 134), diced

Line a colander with muslin and lay the ricotta in it. Set over a bowl, cover and leave to drain for 8-24 hours. Alternatively, put the ricotta in a square of muslin and gather it into a ball. Squeeze firmly to force the water out. Place the cheese in a colander and weigh it down with a plate and a couple of unopened tins. Set aside for 20 minutes, then wring out before you unwrap it.

Turn the drained cheese into a bowl and mash with a fork. Add the eggs, butter, nutmeg and 15g (½oz) of the grated parmesan. Season with salt and pepper then fork through to mix lightly but evenly.

Measure the flour onto a plate. Drop heaped teaspoonfuls of the ricotta mixture into the flour, in batches of five or so. Turn them over with a fork, then remove one by one and gently shake in your hand to form a lightly floured oval. Don't squeeze or press. Place on a lightly floured tray.

Preheat the oven to 200°C (400°F/Gas 6). Put half the parsley butter in a heatproof bowl. Drop the gnocchi, one by one, into a large saucepan of generously salted water, and cook until they float to the surface (about 3 minutes). Remove with a slotted spoon, shaking off excess water, and drop them into the parsley butter. Toss gently to melt the butter, then tip into a medium gratin dish. Dot with the remaining parsley butter and sprinkle with the remaining parmesan. Bake for 10-15 minutes until golden and bubbling.

Toasting before steaming or simmering adds a whole new dimension to couscous. The main thing to bear in mind is that you must season it generously. Herbs, citrus zest, spices and good olive oil will also give the toasted couscous a nudge along in the flavour stakes.

Baked red onions stuffed with spiced couscous

SERVES 4
PREPARATION TIME: 20 MINUTES
COOKING TIME: I HOUR 40 MINUTES

4 large red onions, skin on

2 tablespoons olive oil, plus extra for drizzling

30g (1oz) butter

½ teaspoon ground cinnamon

3 tablespoons couscous

300ml (10½floz) vegetable stock (see page 136) or good-quality bought stock

2 tablespoons chopped dried apricots

2 tablespoons pine nuts, toasted

1 tablespoon chopped flat-leaf parsley

Preheat the oven to 200°C (400°F/Gas 6). Cut the tops off the onions and reserve. Slice any fibres off the root ends of the onions so they can sit upright, but leave as intact as possible so the onions hold together. Place in a baking dish or casserole, pour in a wine glass of water and drizzle with olive oil. Cover with foil or a lid and bake for 1 hour, then uncover and set aside. When just cool enough to handle, scoop out the onion centres with a teaspoon, leaving enough outside layers to form a thick shell. Roughly chop the scooped-out flesh.

Heat the 2 tablespoons of olive oil and 15g (½oz) of the butter in a frying pan. Add the chopped onion plus the cinnamon and couscous. Stir for a few minutes until the couscous turns golden. Add 100ml (3½floz) of the stock, season generously with salt and pepper, and remove from the heat. Set aside for 5 minutes, then add the apricots, pine nuts and parsley and mix well.

Spoon the couscous mixture into the hollowed-out onions in the cooking dish, and pop the onion tops in the dish as well, along with the remaining stock. Dot with the remaining butter and bake for 25 minutes until golden. Cover the onions with foil or a lid if the tops brown too much before the cooking time is up. Serve with the onion tops perched on the onions if you like.

Fried until crisp and golden then braised, these baby eggplants are full of flavour as well as being silky smooth and tender – just as they should be.

Braised baby eggplants with bok choy, peanuts and Thai basil

SERVES 4
PREPARATION TIME: 15 MINUTES
COOKING TIME: 10-15 MINUTES

12 baby eggplants (aubergines), halved lengthways

100ml (3½floz) peanut oil

2 garlic cloves, chopped

3cm (1¼in) piece fresh ginger, finely chopped

6 baby bok choy, halved

4 spring onions (scallions), sliced

2 tablespoons light soy sauce

2 teaspoons palm sugar or soft brown sugar

3 tablespoons peanuts, toasted and crushed

a small handful of Thai basil leaves

Score the flesh of the eggplants in a crisscross pattern, then heat the oil in a large wok until it shimmers. Add the eggplants and fry, turning with tongs, until deeply golden. Transfer to a plate lined with paper towel, then carefully pour most of the oil out of the wok, leaving only about 1 tablespoon behind.

Return the wok to the heat and add the garlic and ginger. Stir-fry for 30 seconds, then add the bok choy and spring onions. Continue to stir-fry for a minute or so more.

Return the eggplants to the wok with the soy sauce, sugar and 2 tablespoons water. Allow to bubble and thicken for a couple more minutes.

Scatter the eggplants with crushed peanuts and Thai basil and serve with steamed rice.

Traditionally, the eggs in this fragrant curry would be hard-boiled but it is far more delicious when they're a little soft inside. To soft boil eggs, cover them with cold water in a saucepan and place over a medium heat. As soon as the water boils, remove from the heat and set aside for 7 minutes. Refresh in cool water.

Malaysian egg curry

SERVES 4
PREPARATION TIME: 15 MINUTES
COOKING TIME: 15 MINUTES

3 vine-ripened tomatoes

1 tablespoon peanut oil

4 French shallots, thinly sliced

3 garlic cloves, chopped

4cm (1½in) piece fresh ginger, finely chopped

1 teaspoon coriander seeds, crushed

1 teaspoon cumin seeds, crushed

½ teaspoon ground turmeric

1 tablespoon sambal oelek

400ml (14floz) tin coconut milk

2 tablespoons tamarind pulp

1 tablespoon palm sugar or soft brown sugar

8 eggs, soft-boiled

2 tablespoons fried shallots, to serve

Cut a shallow cross in the base of the tomatoes with a sharp knife and place them in a bowl. Cover with boiling water and leave for 1 minute. Drain and peel, then roughly chop the flesh and set aside.

Heat the oil in a wok or saucepan, add the shallots, garlic and ginger and cook for 1 minute. Add the coriander seeds, cumin seeds, turmeric, sambal oelek and the chopped tomatoes and sauté for a few minutes more.

Stir in the coconut milk, tamarind pulp and sugar along with a hefty pinch of salt. Bring to the boil, then reduce the heat and simmer for 5 minutes until the mixture thickens.

Add the eggs and simmer for a few more minutes to heat them through. Scatter with fried shallots and serve the curry with steamed rice.

Side dishes

Greens dressed with walnut tarator

Plunge some seasonal greens into salted water and simmer until just tender. Use any type of kale or cabbage, broccoli, silverbeet (Swiss chard) or bok choy. Drain and dress the vegetables with walnut tarator (see page 139).

Green papaya salad

Peel a large green papaya and shred the flesh. Add to a bowl with I large shredded carrot and dress with a few tablespoons of ginger and lime dipping sauce (see page 141). Toss through a couple of spoonfuls of Thai basil leaves, and top with chopped, toasted peanuts or cashews.

Asparagus with brioche crumbs

Cook trimmed green asparagus spears in salted water until just tender. Melt a generous knob of butter in a frying pan and add finely whizzed brioche crumbs with the grated zest of ½ lemon. Stir and toast until golden. Season and scatter over the drained asparagus. You could also serve the cooked asparagus with blender hollandaise or gorgonzola sauce (see page 138).

Red cabbage slaw with gomashio

Slice ½ medium red cabbage very thinly and thinly slice a quartered, cored red apple. Dress with a little toasted sesame oil, soy sauce and rice vinegar. Toss through a few coriander (cilantro) leaves and sprinkle with some gomashio (see page 136). This also goes well with barbecued corn or shredded carrot.

Spiced sweet potato wedges

Preheat the oven to 200°C (400°F/Gas 6). Peel 600g (1lb5oz) orange sweet potatoes, or leave the skin on if you wish, and slice into wedges. Toss the wedges in 3 tablespoons olive oil, 2 crushed garlic cloves, 1 tablespoon each crushed cumin, coriander and fennel seeds and a pinch of chilli flakes. Season and spread out on a baking tray. Bake for 35 minutes or so, turning halfway. Serve the wedges as they are or with parsley or rocket pesto (see page 137).

Beetroot and fig carpaccio

Peel 4 raw beetroot and slice into paper-thin slices. Slice 3 ripe figs as thinly as you can without breaking the flesh. Arrange on a plate and scatter with lemon thyme leaves. Combine 2 tablespoons fig tapenade (see page 138) with 1 tablespoon red wine vinegar, 1 tablespoon extra virgin olive oil and 1 tablespoon water. Spoon over the beetroot and figs and season lightly to finish.

This is nourishing comfort food at its finest. It's a meltingly delicious dish, which has an appealingly sweet combination of flavours that children love, but the addition of some waxy potato would temper it a little. Of course, feel free to vary the root vegetables as you wish.

Shredded vegetable gratin with crème fraîche and gruyère

SERVES 4–6
PREPARATION TIME: 20 MINUTES
COOKING TIME: 1 HOUR

1 garlic clove, halved

soft butter, for greasing

500g (1lb2oz) butternut pumpkin (squash), seeded and shredded

200g (7oz) carrots, shredded

200g (7oz) parsnips, shredded

200g (7oz) orange sweet potato, shredded

400g (14 oz) crème fraîche

100ml (3½floz) dry white wine

120g (4¼oz) gruyère cheese, coarsely grated

2 teaspoons thyme leaves

Preheat the oven to 200°C (400°F/Gas 6). Rub the cut garlic around the inside of a deep, medium-sized gratin dish. Discard the garlic clove and smear the dish with butter.

Place half the shredded vegetables in the dish, pressing down firmly. You can keep the vegetable layers distinct, or mix all the varieties together as you wish. Either way, season the layers well with salt and pepper.

Mix the crème fraîche and wine together and season with salt and pepper. Spoon half this mixture over the vegetables and top with a third of the grated gruyère. Sprinkle with half the thyme, and top with the remaining vegetables, pressing down firmly as before. Pour the remaining crème fraîche mixture over the top, sprinkle with a little salt, pepper and the remaining thyme, and finish with the remaining gruyère.

Cover the dish with foil, seal well and bake for 30 minutes. Uncover, then bake for a further 30 minutes or so until the gratin is golden and bubbling. Remove from the oven and set aside to rest and settle for at least 10 minutes before serving with a salad or steamed green vegetables.

This is a stunning, rustic starter. Should the idea of preparing fresh artichokes fill you with dread, you can use marinated artichoke halves in oil. If you do, simply sauté the shallots and garlic, and stir in the other stuffing ingredients before spooning over the artichokes and baking for 15–20 minutes. You won't need the stock.

Artichokes with lemon and oregano breadcrumbs and citrus mayonnaise

SERVES 4
PREPARATION TIME: 30 MINUTES
COOKING TIME: ABOUT 50 MINUTES

12 young violet artichokes

finely grated zest and juice of 1 lemon

2 French shallots, finely chopped

4 tablespoons olive oil

1 garlic clove, crushed

100g (3½oz) coarse sourdough breadcrumbs

1 tablespoon oregano leaves, chopped

1 glass white wine

1 glass vegetable stock (see page 136) or good-quality bought stock

For the citrus mayonnaise

finely grated zest of 1 lemon

1 tablespoon lemon juice

½ quantity mayonnaise (see page 137) or 120g (4¼oz) good-quality bought mayonnaise

Preheat the oven to 180°C (350°F/Gas 4). Slice the stalks from the artichokes so they will stand upright. Remove the tough outer leaves from each artichoke bud until you reach the lighter-coloured leaves. Cut the spiny tops off the leaves, open the leaves out slightly and use a teaspoon to scoop out the hairy central core or choke, and discard. Drop the artichokes into a bowl of water with the lemon juice added.

In a flameproof casserole dish or sturdy roasting tin, soften the shallots in 3 tablespoons of the olive oil until translucent. Add the garlic and cook for 1 minute. Scoop the mixture into a bowl and add the breadcrumbs, lemon zest and oregano along with some salt and pepper. Mix well.

Remove the artichokes from the water and shake dry. Spoon the stuffing mixture into the cavities between the leaves.

Add the remaining oil to the same casserole or tin and sit the artichokes in it. Pour in the wine and stock and cover tightly with a lid or a double layer of foil. Bake for 30 minutes then uncover and cook for a further 10–15 minutes until the crumbs are golden.

Meanwhile, to make the citrus mayonnaise, stir the lemon zest and juice into the mayonnaise and serve alongside the artichokes.

The ingredients are rich, but this is a delicate dish that's elegant rather than clumsy, thanks to the fine layering. As with all simple food, it demands quality ingredients. Ideally, make your own lasagne sheets, or use sheets of good-quality bought fresh pasta, and roll them out ethereally thin.

Mushroom and basil lasagne

SERVES 6-8
PREPARATION TIME: 40 MINUTES
PLUS INFUSING TIME
COOKING TIME: 50 MINUTES

1 quantity béchamel sauce
(see page 139)

30g (1oz) butter, plus extra for greasing

450g (1lb) fresh lasagne sheets

olive oil, for drizzling

300g (10½oz) mushrooms, any sort, finely chopped

1 garlic clove, crushed

a large handful of basil leaves

4 tablespoons finely grated parmesan cheese

2 balls buffalo mozzarella, torn into pieces

Start by making the béchamel sauce, then cover to prevent a skin forming and set aside.

Preheat the oven to 180°C (350°F/Gas 4) and grease a medium-large ceramic lasagne dish. Cut the lasagne sheets into halves or thirds so they can be layered in the dish easily. Drop each sheet, one by one, into a saucepan of boiling, salted water and simmer for 1-2 minutes, then drain and refresh under cold running water. Drizzle with olive oil and lay the sheets out on clean tea towels in a single layer.

Gently sauté the mushrooms in the butter for a few minutes until softened but not coloured. Stir in the garlic and cook for a further 2 minutes until much of the liquid has cooked off. Spread a little of the mixture over the base of the dish and scatter with basil leaves. Don't use much; this is all about fine and delicate layering, not thick bands of filling. Cover the mushrooms with a layer of pasta, a very thin layer of béchamel, a little seasoning and a sprinkle of parmesan. Top with another layer of pasta then begin layering again, starting with the mushrooms. Continue layering until you have used all the ingredients, finishing with lasagne sheets, béchamel sauce and a final layer of torn mozzarella, all dusted with grated parmesan.

Bake for 35 minutes or so until the lasagne is bubbling and golden at the edges.

Risottos

Bianco

Heat 1 litre (35floz) vegetable stock (see page 136). Finely chop 3 French shallots and soften in 1 tablespoon olive oil and 15g (½oz) butter. Add 400g (14oz) risotto rice and stir to coat the rice. Add 2 glasses dry white wine, stir until evaporated then add a ladleful of stock and a pinch of salt. Stir. As the stock evaporates, add more and stir, continuing for about 18 minutes until the rice is just tender. Take off the heat and stir in 50g (1¾oz) cubed butter and 100g (3½oz) grated parmesan cheese. Cover and set aside for 2 minutes.

Zucchini and taleggio

Make the basic risotto bianco, but stir in a few thyme leaves and 2 trimmed and finely diced zucchini (courgettes) about 15 minutes into the rice cooking time. When the rice grains are just cooked, fold in 100g (3½oz) diced taleggio cheese with the butter and parmesan, and set aside to rest. The cheese will become molten and voluptuous as it warms through.

Tomato and pesto

Make the basic risotto bianco, but stir in 12 roughly chopped slow-roasted tomato halves (see page 42) halfway through cooking the rice. Omit the butter at the end and stir in only 50g (1¾oz) parmesan. Top each bowlful with an extra roasted tomato half and a spoonful of pesto (see page 137) and scatter with basil leaves.

Fennel and lemon

Make the basic risotto bianco, but add a large, finely chopped fennel bulb and a finely chopped garlic clove with the shallots. About 5 minutes before the end of cooking, stir in the finely grated zest of a lemon. When the risotto is cooked, add the juice of a small lemon and replace the butter with an extra 50g (1¾oz) parmesan. Finish with a grating of lemon zest and some chopped fennel fronds.

Wild garlic

Make the basic risotto bianco and just a couple of minutes before the rice is cooked, stir in about 150g (5½oz) wild garlic leaves or baby English spinach. Add the butter and cheese and continue the risotto bianco recipe as written. Serve with extra parmesan.

Cauliflower pangrattato

Make the basic risotto bianco, but add 400g (14oz) cauliflower florets and a bay leaf to the stock. Simmer for 10 minutes. Add 2 crushed garlic cloves to the shallots and include the cauliflower when adding the stock to the rice. Whizz 150g (5½oz) sourdough bread with a garlic clove, a pinch of chilli flakes and 1 teaspoon thyme leaves until crumbs form. Fry the crumbs with 25g (1oz) butter and 2 tablespoons olive oil until golden. Serve the risotto scattered with the toasted crumbs.

Eggplant caviar is also known as 'poor man's caviar', but that's a misnomer. True, you won't find a single fish egg here, but this is still a luxurious mouthful to serve as a canapé, or before a special dinner. And topped with pomegranate jewels, they're as pretty as a picture.

Chervil pancakes with eggplant caviar and pomegranate

MAKES ABOUT 24
PREPARATION TIME: 15 MINUTES
PLUS COOLING TIME
COOKING TIME: 1 HOUR

1 garlic clove

1 teaspoon cumin seeds

2 medium eggplants (aubergines), halved lengthways

3 tablespoons extra virgin olive oil

2 teaspoons pomegranate molasses or a squeeze of lemon

4 tablespoons Greek-style yoghurt

3 tablespoons fresh pomegranate seeds

For the pancakes

225g (8oz) self-raising flour

1 teaspoon baking powder

260ml (9floz) buttermilk

2 eggs, beaten

1 tablespoon chopped chervil or flat-leaf parsley, plus extra leaves to serve

butter, for greasing

Preheat the oven to 200°C (400°F/Gas 6). Use a pestle and mortar to crush the garlic with the cumin seeds and a large pinch of salt. Spread this mixture over the cut surfaces of the eggplants then sandwich the halves together and wrap in foil. Bake for 40 minutes until tender then unwrap and set aside to cool.

Scoop the flesh from the eggplants into a saucepan and discard the skins. Add the olive oil and heat the pan, stirring the mixture as it simmers. Cook for 5 minutes or so to evaporate the excess water and concentrate the flavours. Leave to cool then beat in the pomegranate molasses or lemon juice, 1 tablespoon of the yoghurt and a little salt and pepper to taste.

Combine 2 tablespoons of the pomegranate seeds with the rest of the yoghurt and set aside.

To make the pancakes, whisk the flour, baking powder, buttermilk, eggs and chopped chervil or parsley together until smooth. Grease a hot frying pan with the butter and cook heaped teaspoonfuls of the mixture for 1-2 minutes on each side. Flip them when the little bubbles that rise to the surface start to burst.

Place 1 teaspoon of the eggplant mixture on each pancake and top with a little of the pomegranate yoghurt. Add a few pomegranate seeds and a sprig of chervil to finish.

Miang Kham are traditional Thai snacks and here these delicious parcels have been repackaged slightly to become fresh and elegant canapés or starters. Betel leaves are widely used in cooking and for medicinal purposes throughout Southeast Asia.

Betel leaf wraps with coconut and cashews

MAKES 20
PREPARATION TIME: 20 MINUTES
COOKING TIME: ABOUT 10 MINUTES

50g (1¾oz) fresh or dried shredded coconut, toasted

4cm (1½in) piece fresh ginger, finely chopped

2 red bird's eye chillies, finely chopped

3 tablespoons chopped cashews, toasted

175g (6oz) palm sugar or soft brown sugar

3 tablespoons vegetarian fish sauce or soy sauce

2 tablespoons sieved tamarind pulp or tamarind purée

½ small lime, finely diced, including skin

1 small pomelo, flesh separated and pulled into small chunks

1 French shallot, finely chopped

20 betel leaves or English spinach leaves

a handful of coriander (cilantro) sprouts or leaves

Using a pestle and mortar or a mini food processor, grind half the coconut, half the ginger, the chillies, 2 tablespoons of the cashews and a pinch of salt to a paste. Set aside.

Combine the sugar with 3 tablespoons water in a saucepan and heat gently until dissolved. Increase the heat and simmer for a few minutes until reduced to a syrup. Stir in the cashew paste with the fish sauce or soy sauce. Simmer for 3 minutes more then stir in the tamarind and heat through. Remove from the heat and allow to cool a little.

Mix together the lime, pomelo and shallot. Place the betel leaves on a board, shiny sides down. Spoon 1 teaspoon of the lime mixture onto the centre of the betel leaves then add a little of the cooled tamarind mixture followed by a couple of coriander sprouts or leaves. Pinch each leaf together slightly at the base. You can use a small cocktail stick to secure them if you like.

White asparagus is grown in darkness below the soil surface to keep it blanched of colour, and the resulting spears are delicately flavoured. Some people add sugar to the cooking water to prevent bitterness, but simmering the asparagus in diluted milk has the same effect without the sweetness.

White asparagus with Champagne beurre blanc

SERVES 4
PREPARATION TIME: 10 MINUTES
COOKING TIME: 20 MINUTES

20 white asparagus spears, about 600g (1lb 5oz), trimmed

200ml (7floz) milk

15g (½oz) butter

For the beurre blanc

1 French shallot, finely chopped

4 black peppercorns

1 tarragon sprig

175ml (5½floz) Champagne or dry white wine

175g (6oz) butter, chilled and cubed

Start by making the beurre blanc reduction. Place the shallot, peppercorns, tarragon and Champagne or dry white wine in a saucepan and bring to the boil. Simmer the liquid down slowly for a few minutes until reduced by two-thirds. Strain through a sieve into a heatproof bowl.

Carefully pare away the skin from the asparagus stalks (but not the tips) using a vegetable peeler, treating them gently so the spears don't snap.

Using a frying pan large enough to hold the asparagus in a single layer, lay the spears out flat. Add the milk and 15g (½oz) butter with 200ml (7floz) water to cover the asparagus. Bring to the boil and simmer for 10–12 minutes, turning the spears over occasionally until they are tender. The cooking time will depend on how thick the spears are. Set aside in the pan.

Meanwhile, set the heatproof bowl containing the Champagne reduction over a pan of barely simmering water, being careful not to let the bowl come into contact with the water. Whisk in the cubes of butter, one by one, until emulsified into a smooth sauce. Season with a little salt and pepper. Remove the pan from the heat but leave the bowl over the pan to keep warm, stirring every now and then. The sauce will last for 10 minutes or so like this but any longer and it might split.

Serve the warm sauce spooned over the drained asparagus.

Do buy these golden mushrooms whenever you see them because they are such treasures. Here, they are fried in butter with cherries and wine, and spooned over truffle-spiked potato purée with a few truffle pearls to finish. Truffle pearls are an ingenious vegetarian version of 'caviar' made with black truffle and seaweed.

Pan-fried mushrooms and sour cherries

SERVES 4
PREPARATION TIME: 25 MINUTES
COOKING TIME: 35-40 MINUTES

30g (1oz) butter

1 tablespoon olive oil

2 garlic cloves, crushed

600g (1lb5oz) golden chanterelles, brushed free of dirt

1 small glass Madeira or dry sherry

100g (3½oz) dried sour cherries

1 small glass vegetable stock (see page 136) or good-quality bought stock

1 tablespoon finely chopped flat-leaf parsley

1 tablespoon truffle pearls, to serve (optional)

For the potato purée

900g (2lb) floury potatoes, cut into large chunks

50g (1¾oz) truffle butter or 50g (1¾oz) butter and 2 teaspoons truffle oil

100ml (3½floz) thick (double) cream

To make the potato purée, steam the potatoes over simmering water for 20-25 minutes until completely tender but not falling apart. Pour all the water out of the saucepan and tip the potatoes into it. Place over a low heat for a few minutes, shaking the pan to dry the potatoes.

Press the potatoes through a ricer if you have one – it will produce the smoothest mash – or use a potato masher to crush them until smooth. Beat in the truffle butter (or the butter and truffle oil) and cream. Generously season with salt and pepper. Keep warm.

While the potatoes steam, cook the mushrooms. Melt the butter and oil in a large frying pan over a medium-high heat. Add the garlic and stir, followed by the mushrooms. Toss the pan now and then for a couple of minutes to brown the mushrooms all over. Transfer to a plate with a slotted spoon. Pour the Madeira or sherry into the pan and reduce briskly for 1 minute then add the cherries and stock and continue to simmer for 5 minutes more. Return the mushrooms to the pan, stir in the parsley and season to taste with salt and pepper.

Serve the mushrooms spooned over the potato purée topped with a few truffle pearls (if using).

It's a rare recipe than works as a starter, main or cheese course. Served as a starter or main, a rocket (arugula) side salad wouldn't go amiss. As a dessert or cheese course, the tart will stand alone or can be accompanied by a little crème fraîche. Figs and hard goat's cheese also work extremely well instead of the pears and parmesan.

Pear and parmesan tarte tatin with thyme pastry

SERVES 6-8
PREPARATION TIME: 20 MINUTES
PLUS CHILLING TIME
COOKING TIME: 40 MINUTES

75g (2½oz) light brown sugar

50g (1¾oz) butter

3 tablespoons balsamic vinegar

2 tablespoons chopped walnuts

1 tablespoon thyme leaves

6 ripe but firm pears, quartered and cored

For the pastry

100g (3½oz) butter

200g (7oz) plain (all-purpose) flour, plus extra for dusting

100g (3½oz) parmesan cheese, finely grated

1 egg, beaten

1 tablespoon thyme leaves

To make the pastry, whizz the butter and flour in a food processor until it resembles fine crumbs. Add a pinch of salt and the parmesan and blend for a few seconds. Add the egg and thyme and blitz again until the pastry just comes together into a ball. Knead briefly until smooth, shape into a disc and wrap in plastic wrap. Chill for at least 20 minutes.

Preheat the oven to 180°C (350°F/Gas 4). Heat the sugar in a 25cm (10in) tatin dish or ovenproof frying pan until it melts, shaking and swirling from time to time so it melts evenly. Increase the heat slightly and add the butter and vinegar, allowing the mixture to bubble for a minute or so. Remove from the heat and sprinkle with the walnuts and thyme. Arrange the pears on top, rounded side down, in snug, concentric circles.

On a lightly floured surface, roll the pastry into a circle 2cm (¾in) larger than the dish or frying pan. Using a rolling pin to pick the pastry up, cover the fruit snugly, tucking the edges in to enclose everything securely. Bake for 30 minutes until the pastry is golden and the caramel is bubbling at the edges. Leave to cool for 10 minutes before placing an inverted plate (ideally one with a lip to catch the sauce) on top of the pan. Wearing oven gloves and holding the plate and pan tightly, flip the whole lot over. Remove the pan to reveal the tart, pushing any dislodged pears back into place if necessary.

This is a decadent soufflé cake that will fall and sink slowly as it cools. The middle is dense and mousse-like, the edges crisp and the salted caramel ribbon swirling through the chocolate gives it an edge over any other torte. It's a good idea to make it a few hours in advance, and serve when cool but not chilled.

Bitter chocolate and salted caramel torte

SERVES 12
PREPARATION TIME: 30 MINUTES
COOKING TIME: ABOUT 40 MINUTES

250g (9oz) dark chocolate (at least 70% cocoa solids), in pieces

160g (5½oz) unsalted butter, cubed

175g (6oz) golden caster (superfine) sugar

1 teaspoon vanilla extract

120g (4¼oz) ground almonds

5 medium egg yolks

6 medium egg whites

For the salted caramel

175g (6oz) golden caster (superfine) sugar

120ml (4floz) thick (double) cream

½ teaspoon sea salt flakes

120g (4¼oz) unsalted butter, cubed

To make the salted caramel, pour the sugar into a heavy-based pan and add 3 tablespoons water. Heat gently, stirring only until the sugar has dissolved. Increase the heat to medium-high and allow the syrup to come to the boil undisturbed. Simmer briskly and watch like a hawk until the caramel turns a rich amber colour. Swirl the pan to prevent 'hot spots' but don't stir or the caramel will crystallise. Remove the pan from the heat and carefully stir in the cream and salt; it's sure to hiss and splutter. Now stir in the butter until a smooth caramel forms. Set aside to cool.

Preheat the oven to 180°C (350°F/Gas 4) and line a 25cm (10in) springform cake tin with baking paper. Melt the chocolate, butter and sugar together in a heatproof bowl set over simmering water. (You can melt everything in a saucepan over a very low heat if you prefer, but go gently in case it burns.) Remove from the heat and stir until smooth then mix in the vanilla and almonds, followed by the egg yolks, one by one.

Whisk the egg whites in a clean bowl until they hold stiff peaks. Using a metal spoon, fold 1 large tablespoon of the egg whites into the chocolate mixture to loosen it then fold in the rest, retaining as much air as possible. Scrape into the prepared tin and smooth the top. Pour or spoon the caramel over the top in a big circular swirl, moving from the centre out. Use a skewer or sharp knife to mix the caramel a little deeper into the batter but don't overdo it. Bake for about 30 minutes until puffed up but still wobbly in the centre. Cool completely in the tin before slicing and serving with ice cream or cream.

If an almond tart isn't deep and buttery with a burnished shell, it's just not worth the effort or the calories. There will be no disappointments here with this divine tart, which delivers on every count.

Rich almond tart with red berry compote

SERVES 10-12
PREPARATION TIME: 40 MINUTES
PLUS CHILLING TIME
COOKING TIME: 1 HOUR 20 MINUTES

225g (8oz) plain (all-purpose) flour, plus a little extra for dusting

125g (4½oz) butter, diced

½ teaspoon salt

60g (2¼oz) icing (confectioners') sugar

1 egg yolk

2-4 teaspoons iced water

For the almond filling

250g (9oz) blanched almonds

2 tablespoons plain (all-purpose) flour

250g (9oz) unsalted butter

275g (9¾oz) golden caster (superfine) sugar

1 vanilla bean, split lengthways

4 eggs

300g (10½oz) seasonal berries

For the red berry compote

300g (10½oz) seasonal berries

3 tablespoons golden caster (superfine) sugar

1 tablespoon balsamic vinegar

Preheat the oven to 170°C (325°F/Gas 3). Pulse the flour, butter, salt and sugar in a food processor until the mixture looks like fine breadcrumbs. Add the egg yolk and 2 teaspoons of the iced water, then pulse just enough to bring it all together into a dough. Add 1-2 teaspoons extra iced water if needed. Knead very briefly until smooth, form into a disc and wrap in plastic wrap. Chill for at least 30 minutes. Roll out the pastry on a lightly floured surface until it forms a large enough circle to line a deep 25cm (10in) tart tin with a removable base. Press the pastry into the tin and use a sharp knife to trim off any excess. Chill for at least 30 minutes.

Meanwhile, to make the filling, use a food processor to grind the almonds and flour together until fine. Tip into a bowl and set aside. Add the butter to the food processor along with 250g (9oz) of the sugar and the vanilla seeds (save the empty pod) and mix until light and fluffy. Add the eggs, one by one, with the motor still running, until completely blended. Scrape into the bowl with the almonds and mix well. Scatter the berries on the base of the tart case and spoon the filling over the top. Smooth the surface and sprinkle with the remaining sugar. Bake for 1 hour 20 minutes or so until golden and risen.

Meanwhile, make the red berry compote. Gently heat the berries with the empty vanilla pod, sugar and vinegar until the fruit just starts to bleed its juice. Remove from the heat.

Cool the tart before serving with the compote and crème fraîche.

I find it more effective to make smaller quantities of really special conserves than endless pots of everyday jams that sit sullenly at the back of the cupboard for months. This black fig jam is intensely rich and it's the perfect foil for cheeses, crisp crackers or perhaps with little blue cheese tarts warm from the oven.

Black fig jam

MAKES 2 JARS
PREPARATION TIME: 5 MINUTES
PLUS MACERATING TIME
COOKING TIME: 40 MINUTES

800g (1lb12oz) ripe black figs, halved

½ teaspoon fennel seeds

300g (10½oz) golden caster (superfine) sugar

juice of 1 lemon

Stir the figs, fennel seeds and sugar together in a bowl. Cover and set aside for 4 hours or chill overnight.

Tip the fig mixture into a large saucepan and slowly bring to the boil. Once the mixture has come to the boil, scoop out the figs with a slotted spoon and set aside in a bowl. Increase the heat and simmer the syrup briskly until it reaches the 'hard ball stage' at around 120°C (235°F/Gas ½). If you don't have a thermometer, scoop a tiny amount of syrup out with a teaspoon and drop into a cup of cold water; it should form a hard ball when ready.

Return the figs to the syrup and continue to simmer for about 25 minutes until thickened, stirring occasionally to break up the fruit. Stir in the lemon juice.

Pour the jam into sterilised jars and keep in a cool, dark place.

These delicious butters are more suggestions than rigid recipes, and have many variations. Start with the ideas below, then experiment with different flavours. The butters can be tossed with simple steamed vegetables, cooked pasta, wholegrains and more. You can even freeze them so you have them on standby.

Flavoured butters

MAKES 250G (9OZ)
PREPARATION TIME: 15 MINUTES
PLUS CHILLING TIME

flavourings (see right)

250g (9oz) unsalted butter, softened

I teaspoon sea salt

Beat your choice of flavourings below into the softened butter with the salt. Spoon onto a sheet of greaseproof paper and roll into a cylinder, twisting the ends to seal. Chill for at least I hour to firm up so that you can slice circles off when needed. The wrapped and chilled butters will keep for at least 4 weeks. If you choose to freeze the butter, slice into discs before wrapping the cylinder. Keep the frozen butter for up to 3 months, snapping off a disc as needed.

LIME AND CHILLI BUTTER
Finely grated zest of 2 limes; 2 red chillies, seeded and finely chopped.

BLUE CHEESE AND BLACK PEPPER BUTTER
75g (2½oz) roquefort cheese, finely crumbled; I teaspoon thyme leaves; 2 teaspoons crushed black peppercorns.

GARLIC-HERB BUTTER
2 large garlic cloves, crushed; 3 tablespoons finely chopped basil leaves or chives; 2 tablespoons pine nuts, toasted and chopped.

PARSLEY BUTTER
3 tablespoons finely chopped flat-leaf parsley; ½ garlic clove, crushed; ½ teaspoon crushed black peppercorns.

Basics

Gomashio

Toast 3 tablespoons sea salt in a dry frying pan, stirring often, until it turns grey. Tip into a pestle and mortar, food processor or spice grinder. Toast 400g (14oz) sesame seeds in the same pan until they smell fragrant. Grind the salt and seeds together, by hand or by machine, until broken down but not too smooth or the mixture will become oily. Store in a tightly sealed jar and use within 2 months. Makes I large jar.

Balsamic vinaigrette

Place 4 tablespoons extra virgin olive oil, 2 tablespoons balsamic vinegar, I tablespoon chopped basil, I tablespoon water, a pinch of caster (superfine) sugar and I teaspoon dijon mustard in a mini food processor and pulse until blended. This dressing is especially good with tomatoes and roasted Mediterranean vegetables. For variation, you could also add a whisper of garlic before blending. Makes about 120ml (4floz).

Vegetable stock

Heat I tablespoon sunflower oil in a large saucepan. Slowly brown 2 large sliced carrots and 2 large sliced onions, stirring, for about 20 minutes until the vegetables are golden and caramelised. Add 10 sliced celery sticks, 4 sliced silverbeet (Swiss chard) stalks, 6 bruised garlic cloves, 60g (2¼oz) brown lentils, 3 bay leaves, a small bunch of parsley stalks, I teaspoon sea salt and I teaspoon peppercorns. Pour in 2 litres (70floz) cold water, bring to a simmer and bubble gently for I hour. Strain and discard the vegetables. Return the stock to the pan on the heat and reduce to the desired strength. Makes about 1.8 litres (62floz).

Mayonnaise

Blend or beat 2 egg yolks with 1 teaspoon dijon mustard and a generous seasoning of salt and pepper. As you blend or beat, start to add 275ml (9½floz) very mild olive oil, drop by slow drop. Increase the drops to a thin trickle as you continue to blend. Add half the oil then beat in a good squeeze of lemon juice. Continue adding the oil as before until it has all gone and the mayonnaise is thick and glossy. Taste and add a touch more salt, pepper or lemon juice if needed. To make herb mayonnaise, stir in 2 tablespoons chopped fresh herbs at the end. To make aïoli, crush 2–3 large garlic cloves and add them with the egg yolks. Makes 250g (9oz).

Sweet lemon dressing

Combine 90ml (3floz) olive oil, 1 tablespoon mild honey, the finely grated zest and juice of 1 lemon, 1 teaspoon wholegrain mustard and ½ crushed garlic clove in a screw-top jar with salt and pepper. Shake until thoroughly blended. Robust leaves - witlof (chicory), radicchio, watercress and rocket (arugula) - all bring out the best in this dressing. If you'd rather use a milder leaf, replace the honey with 2 tablespoons finely grated parmesan cheese to pep it up and balance the flavours. Makes about 100ml (3½floz).

Pesto

Roughly chop 1 large garlic clove and add it to a food processor with 60g (2¼oz) pine nuts, a large handful of basil leaves and a pinch of sea salt. Pulse together, scraping down the sides now and then. Add 70g (2½oz) finely grated parmesan cheese and drizzle in 100ml (3½floz) extra virgin olive oil until blended. To make parsley, rocket (arugula) or watercress pesto, replace the basil with your herb of choice and swap the pine nuts with roughly chopped, blanched almonds. To make sun-dried tomato pesto, simply add 5 drained and chopped sun-dried tomato halves with the basil. To make vegan pesto, omit the cheese and increase the pine nuts or almonds to 3 tablespoons. Makes 1 jar.

Fig tapenade

Place 100g (3½oz) chopped dried figs in a pan with 100ml (3½floz) water and simmer for 15 minutes, stirring, until tender. Remove from the heat and cool. Use a pestle and mortar or food processor to crush the figs and liquid with 150g (5½oz) pitted kalamata olives, ½ garlic clove, 2 tablespoons thyme leaves, 2 tablespoons rinsed and drained capers and a twist of black pepper. Pulse and loosen with extra virgin olive oil.

Blender hollandaise

Melt 120g (4¼oz) butter in a small saucepan. Whizz 2 egg yolks in a small blender with 2 tablespoons boiling water and season with a pinch of salt and a little pepper. With the motor on, very gradually trickle in the hot butter until a thick sauce forms. Add a couple of tablespoons of lemon juice and blend again. Taste and add a little more lemon or seasoning before serving if needed.

Gorgonzola sauce

Fry 2 finely chopped French shallots in a little butter until translucent. Add 150g (5½oz) chopped gorgonzola or roquefort cheese and stir gently until the cheese has melted. Stir in 100ml (3½floz) thick (double) cream and mix well. Season with black pepper. A little finely chopped parsley stirred in at the end makes a nice addition. Delicious stirred through pasta.

Walnut tarator

Pulse 200g (7oz) shelled walnuts in a food processor with 1 large crushed garlic clove and a good pinch of salt until quite finely ground. Gradually pour in 2 tablespoons red wine vinegar, 100ml (3½floz) water and 3 tablespoons extra virgin olive oil as you process again to form a creamy but not completely smooth sauce. This Turkish sauce is a bit like a nut pesto and is wonderful with roasted or grilled vegetables.

Best tomato sauce

Peel and halve 1 small onion and lightly bash a whole, peeled garlic clove. Place in a saucepan with 2 x 400g (14oz) tins of good-quality roma (plum) tomatoes and 75g (2½oz) butter or 75ml (2¼oz) extra virgin olive oil. Place over a very gentle heat and slowly simmer, stirring occasionally, for about 40-50 minutes. Season with salt and pepper and discard the onion before using. The garlic will have melted away.

Béchamel sauce

Pour 1 litre (35floz) milk into a pan and add 1 small peeled and halved onion, 10 black peppercorns and 2 bay leaves. Bring to the boil then remove from the heat and infuse for 20 minutes or so. Melt 60g (2¼oz) butter in a pan and add 60g (2¼oz) plain (all-purpose) flour, stirring until a smooth paste forms. Cook gently for a minute or so, stirring, then gradually whisk in the strained milk, beating constantly. When all of the milk has been incorporated, bring to the boil then reduce the heat and gently simmer for a couple of minutes. Season and add a generous grating of nutmeg. Cover to prevent a skin from forming and set aside to cool.

Slow-roasted tomato sauce

Put 300g (10½oz) slow-roasted tomatoes (see page 42) in a food processor or blender with 500g (1lb2oz) tomato passata, a small handful of basil leaves and 2 tablespoons extra virgin olive oil and blend until almost smooth. This is a deep and intense sauce that can be made almost instantly if you have a batch of slow-roasted tomatoes to hand. Add chopped red chilli or crushed garlic before blending for extra flavour. Makes about 720g (1lb9oz).

Horseradish dressing

Whisk 4 tablespoons walnut oil, 2 tablespoons crème fraîche, 1 tablespoon finely grated fresh horseradish (or more to taste), the juice of 1 lemon and a pinch of caster (superfine) sugar together with 2 tablespoons cold water to loosen. Season to taste with salt and pepper. This is strictly for robustly flavoured vegetables and leaves, as it takes a certain strength to stand up to peppery horseradish. Makes 120ml (4floz).

Salsa verde dressing

Chop 1 small bunch flat-leaf parsley and ½ small bunch mint and place in a small bowl. Add 75ml (2¼floz) extra virgin olive oil or enough to cover the herbs. Crush 1 large garlic clove and stir into the herb mixture along with 2 tablespoons chopped capers, 1½ tablespoons dijon mustard and 2 tablespoons red wine vinegar and season with salt and pepper to taste. The sauce should have a spoonable consistency so add more olive oil if needed. Makes about 200ml (7floz).

Satay sauce

Gently fry 1 chopped garlic clove, 2 roughly chopped French shallots and 1–2 roughly chopped red chillies in 1 tablespoon peanut oil until soft but not coloured. Add 2 teaspoons caster (superfine) sugar and 150g (5½oz) toasted and roughly chopped peanuts and cook for 2 minutes until caramelised. Stir in 1 tablespoon soy sauce and 400 ml (14floz) coconut milk and simmer for 5 minutes. Keep the texture chunky, or blend briefly in a food processor. Add the juice of 1 lime and season with a little extra soy sauce if needed. Satay sauce will keep in the refrigerator for 2 weeks or more. Makes about 500ml (17floz).

Ginger and lime dipping sauce

Pour 3 tablespoons boiling water into a heatproof bowl and stir in 1½ tablespoons caster (superfine) sugar until dissolved. Finely chop a 4cm (1½in) piece fresh ginger and 1 large garlic clove and add to the bowl along with 1 seeded and finely chopped red chilli (optional), the juice of ½ lime, 2 tablespoons rice wine vinegar and 2 tablespoons vegetarian fish sauce or soy sauce. Mix well and leave to stand for a few minutes before using. Makes 100ml (3½floz).

Chermoula dressing

Put 1 small bunch coriander (cilantro) and 1 small bunch flat-leaf parsley in a food processor. Add 1 tablespoon toasted cumin seeds, 75ml (2¼floz) extra virgin olive oil, the finely grated zest and juice of 1 lemon, 1 crushed garlic clove, 1 teaspoon ras el hanout, ½ teaspoon paprika and ½ teaspoon salt. Pulse until finely chopped, adding a little more olive oil if it seems too thick. Season with black pepper. Keep covered in the refrigerator for up to 2 weeks. Makes 1 jar.

Index

Published in 2018 by Murdoch Books, an imprint of Allen & Unwin
First published as Vegetarian in 2010 in France by Marabout

Murdoch Books Australia
83 Alexander Street, Crows Nest NSW 2065
Phone: +61 (0)2 8425 0100
murdochbooks.com.au
info@murdochbooks.com.au

Murdoch Books UK
Ormond House, 26-27 Boswell Street, London WC1N 3JZ
Phone: +44 (0) 20 8785 5995
murdochbooks.co.uk
info@murdochbooks.co.uk

For corporate orders and custom publishing contact our business
development team at salesenquiries@murdochbooks.com.au

Publisher: Corinne Roberts
Author: Alice Hart
Photographer: Lisa Linder
Production Manager: Lou Playfair

ISBN 978 1 76063 190 1 Australia
ISBN 978 1 76063 437 7 UK

A cataloguing-in-publication entry is available from the catalogue
of the National Library of Australia at nla.gov.au
A catalogue record for this book is available from the British Library

L&C Printing Group, Cracow Poland